Even the famous and successful have had awkward, embarrassing, difficult, and just plain terrible moments. In this book . . .

- **Carol Burnett** writes about an ill-fated meeting with Cary Grant.
- **Rosie O'Donnell** remembers her inability to express her love for a close girlfriend.
- **Senator Orrin Hatch** regrets voting against Martin Luther King Day.
- **Goldie Hawn** considers her last day on *Laugh-In*.
- **Alan Alda** overprepares for an interview.
- **Ben Stiller** wonders whether he should have stayed in school.
- **Kenneth Cole** gets mixed up during an important speech.
- **Lily Tomlin** reconsiders a wardrobe choice.
- **Arianna Huffington** reveals why she left her first love.
- **Art Garfunkel** fesses up to a missed concert appearance.
- **Liz Smith** reacts badly to a libel attack.

And what do **Shirley MacLaine** and **Paul Newman** regret? You'll have to read to find out. IF I ONLY KNEW THEN . . . is that rare book that could change your life. Don't make the mistake of not reading it!

IF I ONLY KNEW THEN...

Learning from Our Mistakes

Charles Grodin
and Friends and Friends of Friends

SPRINGBOARD PRESS

NEW YORK BOSTON

Springboard Press
Hachette Book Group
237 Park Avenue, New York, NY 10017
Visit our Web site at www.HachetteBookGroup.com

Originally published in hardcover by Springboard Press.

First Trade Edition: April 2009

Springboard Press is an imprint of Grand Central Publishing.
The Springboard Press name and logo are trademarks of Hachette Book Group, Inc.

The Library of Congress has cataloged the hardcover edition as follows:

If I only knew then . . . : learning from our mistakes / Charles Grodin and friends and friends of friends.—1st ed.

    p. cm.
    ISBN 978-0-446-58115-8
  1. Celebrities—United States—Biography. 2. Entertainers—United States—Biography. 3. Politicians—United States—Biography. 4. Attitude change. 5. Common sense. I. Grodin, Charles.
CT220.I4 2007
920.073—dc22   2007009566

ISBN 978-0-446-58219-3 (pbk.)

10 9 8 7 6 5 4 3 2 1

Book design and text composition by L&G McRee

Printed in the United States of America

To my wife, Elissa,
who makes fewer mistakes than anyone I know

Contents

Contents

Contents

Preface

I'm sure more than one person has said, "If you don't get wiser as you get older, then you just get older."

It's always been evident that it's important to learn from our mistakes, since it's inevitable we'll all make some.

I've never understood people who look back on their lives and say, "I wouldn't change a thing." I would, a lot—personally and professionally. I've always changed things based on past experiences, and as a result, as years go by, I'm happier—not as happy as I hope to be someday, but happier.

There are some fascinating stories on the following pages. Some, frankly, I found heartbreaking. Some made me smile, and some made me laugh, but I found all of them compelling. There are also some points of view and conclusions neither you nor I may share.

The idea for this book came from an understanding of how important it is to identify our mistakes, learn from them, and not repeat them. Of course, there can be serious consequences in not learning from our mistakes. Most of us have seen too many people who not only don't learn from their mistakes but are unable to acknowledge they've even made any. It seems they feel that to do so is an admission of weakness instead of strength.

Also, when we've made mistakes in the past, we were unaware of making them, so I have no doubt for most of us that's happening right now, possibly every day. Many people don't give this concept much consideration. *If I Only Knew Then . . .* is an effort to get them to reconsider their lack of consideration.

—*Charles Grodin*

REGIS PHILBIN

Talk Show Host

I had my first talk show in San Diego. It was local and live and late on a Saturday night. I was never that confident about my talent, but I worked hard. I booked the guests, flew them to San Diego, put them up at the Shelter Island Inn, and at 11:45 that night we went on the air. There were no writers, no producers, and no pre-interview. I did the monologue just the way I open my current show, talking about what I had seen and done that week and making it as humorous as I could. The show grew into a monster hit.

One Saturday night the suits came down from Hollywood. My main guest that night was Zsa Zsa Gabor. We had a terrific interview, lots of laughs, and she came off the show giving me a rave to anyone listening backstage. A month later I was in Hollywood to host my own national show. I had a large staff of producers and writers—the type of people I never had in San Diego—but there was a problem, a big one. I was intimidated by all the trappings.

Now other people were booking the guests and writing the jokes, and it was all foreign to me. I wasn't comfortable reading someone else's questions and one-liners. I was too timid to explain that this wasn't the way I was used to doing it. Worse yet, I was replacing the great Steve Allen on his syndicated show for Westinghouse. I considered Steve Allen to be a giant in the business, and I simply could not believe it. I was so nervous, I couldn't sleep.

The opening show was a Monday night in October 1964 with all the confusion and tribulation first shows have, especially with a host hardly anyone had ever heard of. A host who was scared stiff. I stumbled through some jokes in the monologue. Why was I so nervous? I had ad-libbed better stuff than this for three years, just sitting on a stool with no cue cards, and got screams. Suddenly with professional help, I was helpless. The show did get better, even got renewed for another thirteen-week cycle, but soon the executives asked me to come to a meeting at the Beverly Hills Hotel, and they told me the show was canceled. It was a big blow.

What I Learned

With the biggest break of my life I had compromised on important issues and had only myself to blame for the failure of my first national show. I should have insisted on more control. I should have done what I did on my local show. That concept is what got me to Hollywood in the first place. It took a long time to understand that, and there was a lot of heartache along the way. But now, years later, I do my TV show the same way. Yes, there is a co-host, but we do it live. We don't even talk to each other before the show, and it's a success. Whatever your situation, whatever your job, focus on your positives. Build on them. Whatever you do, believe in yourself. If you do that, there's a better chance others will believe in you as well.

CHARLES GRODIN

CBS News Commentator

There's a story I like about a boy who was ten years old and had never spoken. His parents just assumed he was unable to. Then one day at dinner, he tasted the spinach and said, "I don't like this." His parents were stunned.

"Bobby," they said, "you can speak! How come in all these years you've never said anything?" The boy said, "Up until now, everything's been okay."

For me everything seemed okay until I was around fourteen.

If you measure mistakes by the length of time they cause you trouble, then my biggest mistake began then, since to this day I still pay a price for it.

It started innocuously enough. When I entered high school my dad wanted me to help out in his store, where he sold supplies to cleaners, tailors, and dressmakers—things like material, linings, zippers, buttons, and hangers.

He called it the Grodin Company. A "friend" of mine in grammar school used to needle me about my dad's company's name since Dad essentially was the company. From time to time over the years he would have someone working for him, but mostly he worked alone, with the exception of my brother Jack, who was six years older than I was. Jack always helped out in the store whenever asked.

When my time came along at fourteen, I also was willing to help—but only to a degree, and that was the heart of the conflict.

I had started kindergarten at four and Hebrew school at eight, so for as long as I could remember I was in school during the day and spent a few days after school each week in religious training.

When I got into high school I had some other ideas for my after-school time, like athletics and dramatics. I joined the masque and wig club in high school, but I wasn't really available to be in a school play because my dad wanted me to work in his store.

It seemed however much I showed up to help, my dad felt it was not enough. He'd had to drop out of school at thirteen to help support his family. You were allowed to do that in those days, so my dad's idea of work was you get up very early in the morning and you work about a twelve-hour day. That's what he did seven days a week his whole life. Maybe he came home earlier on Sunday some-times, but he worked seven days a week. Not only that, but he did it even though he was always sick.

He developed a rheumatic heart as a boy and was never in good health. The only time he wasn't at work was when he had what seemed to be regular stays in the hospital.

Often he would come home from work and go right to bed so he'd be able to get up and go to work the next day. I have a vivid memory of him sitting at the dinner table, his head leaning on his left hand, exhausted.

I never fully factored in my dad's health in the amount of time I put in at the store. I was so used to seeing him ill that I got used to it. I'd never seen him any other way.

I never realized how serious his condition was. Also, while we weren't rich, I never felt the pressure of not having enough money, and I thought my dad could easily afford to hire a kid who could do what I would do for fifty cents an hour, which he often did.

Still, Dad felt it should be me there more often and not some other kid.

This conflict had a couple of noticeable results. I was just about never given the family car to drive after I got my license at sixteen, and my dad eventually wanted me to put all requests for *anything* in writing, which I did. He would respond in writing as well, even though we lived together in a small six-room house!

He just didn't want the stress of having to deal with me in person in any situation where we had differences. In spite of all of this, though, there was never any doubt that my dad and I loved each other very much.

Later, when I was older and working at the store, more than one customer would say, "Oh, you're the one who wants to be an actor. Your dad is always talking about you." In spite of our differences, I got the feeling my dad was proud of me.

My mom later told me that Dad was shocked and so happy that it was his wayward son who as valedictorian gave the commencement speech at his high school graduation.

I remember one time when I was about ten, before all our trouble started, Dad standing at a railroad station, leaning down and kissing me on the cheek before he and my mom left for a rare vacation.

Then one day my dad suddenly died.

He was in the hospital, which, again, wasn't unusual, and I was alone in the store when I got a call from my mother to come to the hospital right away, as my dad wasn't expected to live through the day.

Astonishingly, the thought of my dad dying had never even occurred to me. I was in complete shock as I raced to the hospital. I had the car that day.

When I got to his room, he was in the then familiar oxygen tent—in those days what looked like a plastic tent was put over the patient. He was weak but conscious, and I just stood there as we looked at each other. I didn't speak, and he couldn't.

I went home and completely fell apart. Soon, I got the call. He died at five minutes to five on June 26, 1953. He was fifty-two and I was eighteen. I have never really recovered.

While I've been able to have a relatively happy life, my dad's sudden passing has haunted me. I've replayed the events and wondered how much I contributed to his early death.

If I had been more cooperative, would he have lived a long life?

No. Might he have lived longer? Yes. Was I wrong not to have helped more? Yes.

I always tried to make my case to myself by saying I wanted to finally have my free time after school and my dad could afford to hire another kid to help.

That's all true, except for one thing. I never really considered the emotional price he was paying for my willfulness, and if I had it to do over I would have been there at the store with him as much as he wanted. If I had it to do over, which, of course, sadly, I don't.

WHAT I LEARNED

If you have a conflict with someone you love, really consider how he or she feels as much as you can, even if you don't agree.

You need to, first and foremost, do what you believe is right, but sometimes giving a lot of thought to what a loved one feels will significantly affect what you believe is right.

Sometimes getting your way really isn't worth it.

CAROL BURNETT

Actress, Author

Cary Grant?"

Harvey grinned and nodded.

"CARY Grant?"

More grinning and more nodding from Harvey.

"*The* Cary Grant?"

Harvey's head was bobbing up and down so hard, I thought it would fly off and go bouncing all around the rehearsal hall.

"How? When?"

We were gathered around the big table for our regular Monday-morning reading of that week's show. Vicki, Tim, Lyle, the guests (I don't remember who), our director, Dave Powers, and I were all glued to Harvey's story about the weekend party he had attended in Beverly Hills.

"Okay: It was Saturday night, and *he* was there! Naturally, he was gorgeous, charming, funny, and get this . . . interested in *me!* He never misses watching our show. In fact, he asked the hostess if she'd mind if he disappeared for an hour when ten o'clock rolled around because we were on that night and he doesn't like to miss our show."

I tried catching my breath. "Omigod—you mean Cary Grant actually *knows* who we are?"

"He went on and on about how much he loves the show and how much we make him laugh."

All of us were silent for a bit.

Wow. Cary Grant . . . a *fan*. The idea was overwhelming. I remembered his movies, and my grandmother, Nanny, saying, "He's the second most beautiful thing in the world next to Hedy Lamarr." I thought he was beautiful too, but I also thought he was funny. He could do great "takes" and body-pounding pratfalls (in his earlier movies) . . . an athlete, and a hilarious one. Charm, of course, oozed out of his pores. And now, by golly, *he* knew of *my* existence. Ain't show biz grand?

A few weeks later my husband, Joe, and I were invited to a cocktail party at Peggy Lee's house. She had been a guest on our show a few times and we'd grown pretty friendly. Joe and I were the first ones to show up. My fault—I never could stand being late to anything. Our coats were hung up in the hall closet, and I began making friends with the caterer. It wasn't long before Peggy appeared, looking beautiful in an elegant hostess gown. In a few minutes the doorbell started ringing in earnest, and it wasn't long before the place was wall-to-wall with celebrities. I always mentally pinched myself over how lucky I was to actually know all these talented folks! The party was in full swing— Alan King keeping everyone in stitches, hors d'oeuvres being cleaned off the trays before they made it clear around the room, Frank Sinatra's "Come Fly with Me" swinging through the speakers. And then, suddenly the whole party quieted down and all heads were turned to the front door. I looked.

Cary Grant.

Peggy ran to greet him. Taking his elbow, she led him into the room, and people began to make a path so they wouldn't have to wiggle in and around the guests. She was introducing him to those who had never had the honor. Even the biggest stars all but genuflected. He was very much at ease, laughing and shaking hands, and as they got nearer I bolted for the coat closet. Joe was at my heels: "What're you doing? Don't you want to meet Cary Grant?"

"No."

My coat . . . my coat. Here it was . . . Please, God, get me outta here.

"Are you nuts? All you've been talking about is Harvey's story, and here he is! Here's your chance!"

I had my coat on. "Let's go."

"Will you please tell me what the hell's the matter with you?"

Poor Joe. He just didn't get it. "Poor Joe, you just don't get it." I had to explain: "Look, he *likes* me! He makes it a point to watch our show every single week! You think I want to spoil that?"

"Why would you spoil it?" I had always thought Joe was smarter than that.

"Because I wouldn't know what to say, or how to act, and I would make a fool of myself, and he wouldn't like me anymore! Okay? Let's go home!"

We hadn't yet reached the door when I felt the tap on my shoulder. I turned around and there they were: Peggy and Cary.

Peggy said, "Carol, where're you goin'? You can't leave yet—Cary's dying to meet you!"

Oh, gee. I looked up into his face . . . *that face* . . . and I forced a lame smile. He took my hand and his mouth started moving. Trouble was, I couldn't *hear* him! My heartbeat was so loud, I thought my ears were going to implode. Watching his lips move, I just knew what he was saying had to be the most charming sentences anyone had ever uttered, but I couldn't *hear*.

He kept on and on . . . holding my hand . . . sometimes even squeezing it a little. I thought he'd never stop. Oh, but then he did . . . his mouth had stopped moving. Oh, God, it's my turn now. He's waiting for me to say something . . . *anything*.

Then it came out in a rush. "You're a credit to your profession."

Why didn't the floor open up? Why didn't someone distract him before I opened my mouth? Why didn't we make it to the door in time? Why did we go to the party in the first place? Why was I born?

On the way home in the car, Joe looked at me and said, "You were right."

What I Learned

Trust your instincts.

GOLDIE HAWN

Actress

Good morning, Miss Hawn," the security guard greets me cheerfully as I pull into the NBC parking lot for the last time.

"Morning, Jim," I reply with a smile that doesn't quite reach my eyes.

Steering my maroon Chevrolet Corvette into the slot marked by a sign on the wall reading LAUGH-IN: GOLDIE HAWN, I head with a heavy heart for the door I have opened every working day for the last three years, in beautiful downtown Burbank.

As I walk down that long, long corridor to the studio, passing people I have come to know and love, I can hardly believe I am leaving the show today. Peering in through every doorway, I am wistfully aware of how much I have taken everything for granted. Five days a week, I have walked this corridor without thinking. Now I really look at the stages, the rehearsal halls I've worked in, the room where my bikini-clad body was painted with words and symbols, the newsroom.

Passing Hank, the funny makeup man, the one I joked with all the time about the double chin he insists I don't have, I wave and giggle. I pass Tom Brokaw, the new NBC anchor, who greets me each morning with a smile and a bright hello. I must admit I have a bit of a crush on him.

Looking into one rehearsal hall, I remember the day I danced there in a tight red sweater jumpsuit. I glanced up and could hardly believe my eyes. Elvis Presley had wandered in to watch us rehearsing.

I stop, soaking up the memory now, and still taste how it felt to see the King standing there, emitting such incredible sexual energy, I thought I was going to swoon just being in the same room. That man and his music made my teenage hormones rage. Despite my promises to my father to listen to only classical music, I lived head to toe for rock and roll.

Elvis was introduced and walked over to me, reached out, and touched my tousled hair. "Why, Goldie," he said, smiling that crooked smile of his, "no wonder you're so funny. You look like a chicken that's just been hatched."

Walking on down the corridor, I remember the time we all chased George Schlatter, the producer and director of *Laugh-In*, when he had us working on a sketch until three in the morning. Dick Martin, Dan Rowan, Ruth Buzzi, and I were dressed in overalls, supposedly to paint a wall, but it was so late and we were so tired and none of us wanted to get covered in paint. With one look, we yelled, "Get George!" instead. We chased him down this hallway with rollers dripping paint until he ran upstairs and locked himself in his booth.

Turning down a side corridor into the *Laugh-In* hallway, the place where our little family gathers every week, I step into my dressing room, which looks just the same as it always has. There is the old telephone, the bowl of fresh fruit, the makeup table, and the ugly brown couches. Only now they don't look so ugly anymore.

What I Learned

Try to fully appreciate what you have when you have it. Nothing is forever.

ALAN ALDA

Award-Winning Actor, Bestselling Author

One of my charming failings is that I don't mind if people think I'm smarter than I am. I guess, actually, this is only charming to me, but I usually find it captivating.

This little idiosyncrasy rose up to bite me one day, though, and it didn't bite me in private, where nobody would notice; it took a chunk out of me while I was in front of a television camera.

For eleven years I hosted a show on public television called *Scientific American Frontiers*. I got to interview scientists from all over the world; hundreds of them. And it was a feast for me. As they worked on unraveling the mysteries of nature, it was like listening to a detective story told by Sherlock Holmes himself. Sometimes they would tell me about an invention that was limited in scope, such as a device that helped you lift heavy weights, and I could ask questions that were sensible and not too far-reaching. But sometimes the area of the scientist's interest was much broader.

Early in the run of the show, I was set to interview Carl Sagan and I realized suddenly that we wouldn't be talking about a device in a lab. I was going to be asking him about the whole cosmos. I was a little scared. Where would I begin? "So how did this universe thing get to be like this? Where did all this stuff come from?" Somehow, I needed to start off a little smarter than that. I read everything I could that Sagan had written. I had been doing this with all the scientists I met, but with Sagan I piled it on. And I had to cram, because I only had a couple of weeks before we'd talk.

We met Sagan in front of his house at Cornell University. As we walked down the path to his front door I could see a huge, crashing waterfall in a gorge a hundred feet below us. It was dramatic and exciting, and it mimicked the rush of thoughts in my head. I had filled my brain with big bangs, expanding universes, extraterrestrials, gravity, black holes, asteroids, and a few other things that didn't quite fit. Shreds of knowledge attached themselves to one another and re-formed into cockeyed notions, but I was eager to talk with Sagan, and I knew I could rely on his experience at being interviewed to get us through.

We sat down to talk in the airy, sunlit office where he did his writing. He was congenial and responsive, and everything seemed to be going well until we got to the subject of the expanding universe. Many years earlier, when I had first read that the universe was expanding, I picked up a pencil and wrote in the margin of the book I was reading, "This must be like a ball being thrown in the air over and over. It goes up and comes down again." I was sure that if the universe expanded, eventually it would run out of steam; gravity would start to pull it back again until there was another big bang. It seemed to me it was like respiration: every universe would have a life of one breath. This is a nice idea, and it might make some kind of poem. It might even make a question in a conversation with a scientist, but it's not a very good *assumption* to make, and it certainly is not something that you want to try to maneuver Carl Sagan into agreeing with. I didn't even ask him if anybody else had ever thought of this idea. I just thought if I moved him in the right direction, he'd tell me that that's the way he saw the cosmos too and I would be really smart.

I didn't know it then, but physicists *have* thought of this clever idea. Unlike me, they also have the ability to add up all the stuff in the universe and they figured out it doesn't add up to a bouncing ball. I noticed a slight unfocusing of his eyes as I cheerfully danced down this path. *Is he stunned*, I thought, *that I see so deeply into the cosmos?*

After a couple of hours the interview was over. He was probably exhausted, but I was exhilarated. I'd had an actual conversation about astrophysics with a real astronomer. The producer of the show invited me out for a cup of coffee before we met with the next scientist. I didn't want to gloat about how well it had gone with Sagan, and I was ready to respond to his praise modestly. Instead, his eyes drilled into mine and he said in a very direct way, "I've been wondering why you were showing off. I'm surprised you would do that."

My ears burned with anger. *Showing off?* What was he talking about? I was trying to be up to the job.

He didn't stop there. Why hadn't I just asked questions as if I didn't know the answers, he asked, and let Sagan be the smart one?

My ears burned for another day or so, and then it finally sank in. All the preparation I was doing, reading everything the scientists had written, was making me ask questions that I thought revealed a knowledge of their work, but it only got in their way. My questions were based on assumptions that left them no room to tell their own story. After that day with Carl Sagan, I began to go into interviews with little or no preparation, which forced me to ask truly basic questions. This way I could let the scientists explain their experiments from the ground up—now that I was willing to look as dumb as I actually was. And suddenly, something happened between us. They were talking to me in a way they never had before. I was hearing about a universe I had only imagined, but which they had seen. I was letting in reality, and it was thrilling.

WHAT I LEARNED

I got smarter by being dumber. That was a surprise.

My afternoon with Sagan started me off on a journey on which I discovered that there are actually several levels of ignorance. And I've done time on all of them. The rudimentary level is simply not knowing anything and keeping quiet about it. This is the blissful level. You don't bother anyone else and they don't bother you. A lower rung of ignorance hell is "knowing" something that's not so—and then telling everybody else about it. An even lower rung, and maybe the most dangerous, is thinking that what you know, whatever it is, even if it's right, is all there is to know. That's where I was with Sagan. I was enjoying my little smattering, and I thought it put me in a position to frame complex questions.

The elevator up out of this hell was an easy one to take. All I had to do, I found out, was to *listen*. What an idea.

I began to see that no matter how much I thought I knew, if I actually listened to what other people were saying, I would wind up knowing more. Even if I thought I knew more than they did. Because letting other people in always led to hearing what was behind what they were saying. Somewhere in them there was something valuable that I would miss if I stopped them and made them check their forbidden ideas at the door.

What I learned is that nothing beats listening. Real listening leads to questions instead of oratory.

And, suddenly, I got it. I'd been doing it all along; I'd been doing it on the stage, but not in life. I'd learned as an actor that listening isn't just waiting for my cue, for the moment when I get to talk. Listening is letting the other person change me. On the stage, I always let what the other person says force me into saying my next line. I don't say it because it's written in the script; I say it because this person has forced it out of me. And when I listen in life now, thanks to that moment with Sagan, I try to leave myself open, to listen closely, without defenses. And if I don't like what I'm hearing, sometimes I actually remind myself, *Maybe this person can change me.* And then I hear stuff I never heard before.

BEN STILLER

Actor, Director, Producer

I have made many mistakes in my life. Probably one of the biggest was quitting college. I started making my own home movies when I was about ten: Super 8mm epics made with my friends on 84th Street and Riverside Drive. The films usually involved murder and some form of revenge. We were probably inspired by *Death Wish* and other gritty seventies fare we were watching at way too young an age. So movies were what I always wanted to do, and I knew it.

School was never ever something I liked. From kindergarten on, through grade school, I went against the norm. I remember not liking being assembled into a group. It felt like we were being imprisoned or institutionalized in some way. Once when I was talking to a friend during an assembly in second grade, the teacher in charge, Mr. Shild, asked me in front of everyone at the school, "Benjamin, did you hear me, or have you not washed out your ears today?" That was it. I was personally devastated and after that never really got with the program.

High school was even worse. So when it came time to go to college, I was already lobbying my parents to let me stay in New York and try my hand at acting and directing movies. But there was one school I would consider: USC film school, to which every aspiring filmmaker aspired. I went and visited with my dad. It seemed like another universe, where the students lived on a higher plane. I also remember there was a Sizzler across Martin Luther King Jr.

Boulevard, where I sat with my dad and realized that this was the place I belonged. Of course I didn't get in. I don't know if it was grades, or that my application lacked any sort of spark, or probably both.

After that, the only other place I wanted to go to was UCLA. They had a good film program too, but it didn't start until junior year, so I enrolled in the acting program to bide my time till junior year, when I would tear it up. I lasted seven and a half months. Perhaps it was the huge size of the place—I was used to a small high school in New York City that had about a hundred students. My first history class at UCLA had 350. Also, at my high school we didn't have homerooms. We had "clusters" (it was progressive), and we called the teachers by their first names. Not at UCLA. I was terribly intimidated and lonely too. But I did have a great roommate, a girl who was a junior and so nice to me. She was basically the only person I hung out with

I got in a production of *The Resistible Rise of Arturo Ui*, in which I had about five lines. That was exciting but ended quickly. My most gratifying college experience was being an intern on *Thicke of the Night*, a short-lived talk show hosted by Alan Thicke. I got to drive him around a few times, walk Charlton Heston to his car, and stuff like that.

Meanwhile, I was plotting my escape. I wrote my folks a letter explaining that I needed to come back to New York to start auditioning and taking acting classes, that this whole college thing was a waste of time. I know they didn't want me to quit, but I was really adamant. So I sold my slate-gray metallic Rabbit and flew home on the red-eye the night after my last exam for third-quarter classes. I think it was March of '84.

I got home to my folks' apartment on the Upper West Side. It was about 7:00 a.m. I think they were still sleeping. I walked down the long hallway to my room. It had been converted to a "guest suite" already. I plopped down on my suitcase, looking out the window over the rooftops of the brownstones to the west. I thought, "Finally, no more homework. Ever! No more school, ever again for the rest of my life. I am free to do whatever I want to do." I heard the clinking of the old radiator pipe from my bathroom. A sort of chill came over me as I looked out at the cold gray sky. Now what?

What I Learned

Sometimes, you need to embrace where you are, even if it is not the most comfortable place. I was impatient when I was young, always wanting to get to the next experience. But in reality, I couldn't get there till I was ready to get there. I missed out on a part of my youth—the college years, the time in your life when you have a chance to find your independence without the pressure of having to succeed in the real world. I wish I had stayed in college. The next few years, in essence, ended up being my college experience, only not in college but living at home and working in New York.

Someday I think I might go back to school.

JOHN GABRIEL

Soap Opera Star

I played the role of Dr. Seneca Beaulac for ten years on the highly successful soap opera *Ryan's Hope*.

I'd played the same character for so long that people would sometimes ask me if Dr. Beaulac ever crept into my real life. It only happened once.

I went with a couple of friends to see Sylvia Syms, a very talented singer, at the Algonquin Hotel in New York. It was a wonderful act. She was a pal of Sinatra's and her show was a homage to him. She had just finished and had come back for her encore. As Sylvia was about to introduce the musicians, she paused for a moment and, without warning, fell like a rock to the floor. There was about ten seconds of absolute silence. The audience was stunned. We didn't know if her collapse was part of the act or if it was for real.

Now, I'd had three rather large glasses of cabernet, and my character on the soap was in the middle of a story that required me to spend weeks in the emergency room as Dr. Beaulac, brilliant MD. These factors partially explain my next move.

I jumped up (Dr. Beaulac to the rescue) and ran to the still unconscious singer. As soon as I arrived, of course, I realized I didn't have a clue as to what to do. There wasn't a cue card in sight. I asked with desperation if there was a doctor in the house. There was, but it was no help to poor Sylvia. According to the doctor she was gone as soon as she hit the floor. He assumed it was a massive heart attack.

WHAT I LEARNED

As an actor it's important to believe that you're the character, but it's best to confine that belief for the camera.

GENE WILDER

Actor, Writer

Jerome Robbins was going to direct Bertolt Brecht's play *Mother Courage* on Broadway, with Anne Bancroft as the star.

Mr. Robbins wanted to audition as many actors from the Actors Studio as he could, and since Cheryl Crawford, one of the founders of the studio, was producing the play, it was easy. (She was the one who got me in, along with Elia Kazan.)

I read for the small but very good part of Swiss Cheese, Mother Courage's son. I memorized the scene I was supposed to read, as I always did, and found a "character jacket" to wear. The audition went so well that Mr. Robbins asked me to come back the next day and read again. The second audition went so well that he asked me to study the part of the chaplain, which was one of the leading roles.

I memorized the scene he wanted me to read, found another character jacket, and also brought a prop (a hammer or a broom, I forget which) so that I could be doing something instead of just standing there saying lines.

The audition went well. Mr. Robbins asked me to come back the next day and audition again. This turned out to be a habit of Jerome Robbins's, to keep actors auditioning so that he could be sure, and also, *I'm* sure, so that he could get ideas for how to direct certain scenes. (According to Actors Equity, you're supposed to pay an actor after three auditions, which Mr. Robbins never did.)

After my fifth audition I was told that I would have to do one more *final* audition. The competition for the role was between me and a wonderful actor named Gerald Hiken. By this time my confidence had dropped a few notches. The horrible trap is that an actor tries to remember what he or she did that impressed the director originally, and then, unfortunately, the actor starts imitating what he thought he did. Nevertheless, after my sixth audition I got the part.

Rehearsals were a little strained. Mr. Robbins thought that the best way to get us into Brecht's Communist/Socialist way of thinking was for all of us to play Monopoly during our lunch hour. I should have known that there was trouble ahead.

We opened previews at the Martin Beck Theater to a packed house. I had a rousing and funny scene toward the end of the first act, after which Mother Courage and her daughter and I pushed Mother Courage's wagon to our next destination (on a revolving stage), accompanied by some thrilling music. Before the curtain could come down, the audience burst into applause. But Mr. Robbins cut the heart of the scene the next day. He said, "That isn't what Brecht wants. It's the intellectual ideas that he's trying to get across, not the conventional emotion that we get in American plays." (My father would have said, "Was you there, Charley?")

Jerome Robbins found a patsy in every production—someone he could pick on if he was frustrated with how things were going. (Many famous directors have been guilty of the same habit—Otto Preminger and John Dexter, to name two.)

Robbins had selected a wonderful actor by the name of Eugene Roche to be his patsy. One afternoon, when everything Mr. Robbins was doing seemed to make things worse, he started in on Eugene in front of the rest of the cast. We all had to stand there and listen to Jerry Robbins railing and belittling—until he crossed the line. Eugene, who was a devout Catholic with five children, stood up and said:

"Listen, you little fuck—if you insult me one more time, I'm going to come over there and smash the teeth out of your fucking face."

From that time on, Eugene Roche became Jerome Robbins's favorite actor.

The whole *Mother Courage* experience felt like a big mistake.

After the previews began, Anne Bancroft asked me if I would like to meet her boyfriend, who came to pick her up each night after the show. I said, "Yes, I would love to meet him." The boyfriend's name was Mel Brooks.

WHAT I LEARNED

Occasionally, out of a horrible experience a blessing may come.

KITTY CARLISLE HART

Actress, Singer, Champion of the Arts

As far back as I can remember, and I'm now ninety-six, I never really cooked anything. When I was growing up in Shreveport and New Orleans, we always had wonderful cooks, and having spent my teens in Europe, I always enjoyed good food whether dining in or out, and when I married Moss Hart we had even better cooks. Some of the chattering class even said Moss married me because I could speak French to the maître d's.

I will never truly understand what possessed me, but one year I agreed to cook Thanksgiving dinner for Moss and my two small children in the country all by myself. "The country" was Long Beach Island, New Jersey, where we spent many wonderful summers, albeit with cooks and butlers and maids. This Thanksgiving would be *en famille*. (Other than to maître d's, Moss hated it when I spoke French because he felt left out, but I thought it was good for *les enfants*.)

Now, "cooking" Thanksgiving dinner actually meant that our miraculous Alma (the real cook) would prepare everything ahead of time—that is, stuff the turkey, wrap it in bacon and buttered cheesecloth, prepare all the side dishes in casseroles, and so on. All I really had to do was put the bird in the oven and warm up the sides and the gravy. The four of us drove down to Long Beach Island for the first time in our lives without butlers and cooks and maids, and marveled at how much fun we were having *en famille*, and how we were starting a tradition and would never have Thanksgiving any other way. We arrived with plenty of time to enjoy the early-afternoon sun at the shore, and for me to get the bird in the oven. I sent Moss and the children out to the beach for a long walk to get their appetites going.

While they were away I put the bird in the oven, set the table, arranged all the sides and gravy on the stovetop, and took a short nap. When Moss and the children arrived back from their walk, everyone marveled that I had set the table all by myself, and how good the house smelled. "Sit down, I'll serve," I announced, and went back into the kitchen. I checked all the vegetables and gravy. Everything was perfect. I opened the oven door to pull out the turkey. I knelt down on the floor to get a better look at it. To my surprise, the bird was still perfectly white, covered with the same white buttered cheesecloth. It was the Moby Dick of turkeys. Though I had carefully set the temperature of the oven to Alma's specifications, I had forgotten to actually turn the oven on.

And that is how my family found me, on the floor in the kitchen, my face in the oven, whimpering. We spent that Thanksgiving night under the orange roof of a Howard Johnson's and promised to tell Alma that her instructions and her bird were the best we'd ever had.

And of course I never had to cook anything ever again.

WHAT I LEARNED

The more inexperienced you are, the more careful and thorough you have to be, and that applies to cooking a turkey and everything else in life.

MARY STEENBURGEN

Actress

W hen asked by my friend Charles Grodin to write about a mistake I made, I knew that I would have no problem thinking of plenty to write about. After all, upon meeting my best friend, I stated, "I have nothing in common with her," and the love of my life, Ted Danson, was someone whom I judged so severely that I wasn't even very excited about the prospect of working with him. I have a huge history of being wrong. But the story that I am going to tell is one that has haunted me, and it is something that I reflect back on when I tend to lose my way.

My dad was a sweet, strong angel of a man. He was a man of few words, but we respected him so much that when he did speak, we all listened. He was a freight train conductor for the Missouri Pacific Railroad, but he had heart problems and so he was not able to work for years at a time. He would try to do odd jobs to help support our family. One time he got involved with a shoe company. They sold shoes by using traveling salesmen to help their customers order shoes through a catalog. The company sent my father a sign to put on the back of his car that said HANOVER SHOE SALESMAN.

It was an old secondhand car, and between the sign and the condition of the car, I wasn't too keen on driving around with my father. I was thirteen and suddenly aware of our lack of money compared to the wealth of the rich kids at school. I mostly walked home from school, but this one day my father came to pick me up. As we were driving away from the school I saw this boy, Charles Harrison, who was president of our class and the most popular guy in our grade. I didn't want him to see me in our embarrassing car, so I ducked down and pretended to tie my shoes.

There was silence for a moment and then my father softly said, "Mary, you don't have to be ashamed of this old car."

That's all he said.

What I Learned

Years later, I can still hear the sound of his sadness and feel my face burn with shame at my own snobbery. I think that this tiny little moment actually informed a lot about the way I have dealt with the many blessings that have come my way. I am deeply proud to be a trainman's daughter from Arkansas, and I have been vigilant to remember what does and doesn't matter in life.

ORRIN G. HATCH

United States Senator

Y ou can't serve in politics for as long as I have without making a good number of mistakes.

I'm sure my critics have a long list of mistakes that I've made; some might be justified and some not. But my list is much different from theirs. They look at the issues I have championed that they opposed, or the times when I forged a compromise when they thought compromise was not an option. The mistakes on my list are more personal—people I may have hurt, missed opportunities with my family, or difficult experiences that molded my character.

One of the worst decisions I have made as a senator, though, was my vote against making Dr. Martin Luther King Jr.'s birthday a national holiday.

I admired Dr. King for his amazing success in leading the cause of freedom and the constitutional right to individual civil rights. He was by far the most influential African American leader since the abolition of slavery and one of the greatest men of the twentieth century.

But I convinced myself that there were valid reasons to vote against the holiday. While he was a great leader who deserved to be revered for generations, I could think of other great men in our nation's history who did not have commemorative holidays— Thomas Jefferson, Alexander Hamilton, Franklin Delano Roosevelt, Frederick Douglass, and Booker T. Washington, to name just a few. Why, I argued, should we ask taxpayers to pay $1 billion a year in lost productivity, as no work is being done by so many, to elevate Dr. King above any of these other historical figures? I figured we had enough federal holidays.

I voted against the holiday, a vote that I will never get to rectify. A vote that has tugged at my conscience throughout my career.

What I Learned

What I failed to realize at the time was that this holiday was more than just celebrating the life of one man. Dr. King represented the courage, conviction, and dedication of millions throughout America who had sacrificed themselves and even their lives for racial freedom.

I learned that legislation often goes beyond cold policy calculations, and Congress has a responsibility to consider the impact that policy will have on real people. So many Americans had an emotional and spiritual bond with Dr. King because they had felt the sting of discrimination and prejudice. They stood with him, fought intolerance with compassion, hatred with love, and violence with peaceful disobedience. Together, they secured America's promise of freedom and opportunity for all in America, regardless of their race or any other discriminatory factor.

ROBERT ELLIS

Real Estate Executive

When my son was nine years old, I became a soccer coach for his team. This turn of events was orchestrated by my wife. When she found out all the league entries were taken, she told the authorities, "But my husband is a coach." That certainly opened the door for my son. When she told me what she had done, her next question was "Do you know anything about soccer?" The answer was no, absolutely zero.

I approached the assignment as though I were coaching a professional team. The next year was filled with books on soccer; going to clinics; meeting Juan Mazia, Pelé's coach; and even meeting Pelé.

One day after having practices three days a week, giving lectures to the team that would make Knute Rockne and George Patton proud, I asked, "Are there any questions?" One boy raised his hand and said, "My brother got a goldfish for his birthday." It suddenly hit me that the kids had never been in organized sports before. They wanted to have fun. To get them to a more skillful level, I had to take it slow and easy. I wanted to be the total opposite of the bullying coach who abuses the authority he's given.

One of the boys became a team captain or assistant coach. He could talk to the others on their level. After each game, I called every kid on the phone to encourage him and thank him. Parents' suggestions were accepted, and many parents participated. Practices became fun—it wasn't all soccer talk.

WHAT I LEARNED

I learned more from my young players than they ever learned from me.

I learned how to listen and to value other people's opinions no matter what their age, and this serves me well in all parts of my life.

Kids nine to ten years old have not developed total physical strength and coordination, so we worked on developing mental skills. Since we had practices three days a week, more than any other team, we should be better. They believed it, and, quite frankly, so did I. We went on to have five out of eight seasons with undefeated teams.

ARIANNA HUFFINGTON

Journalist, Author

I was twenty-one when I first met Bernard Levin on a panel for *Face the Music*, a British guess-the-music TV show. He was forty-two. I was there as a curiosity—a young woman with a foreign accent, elected president of the Cambridge Union. He was there as the celebrated columnist for the *Times*, an intellectual with an encyclopedic knowledge of music and pretty much everything else. Except me. He knew nothing about me. But I knew a lot about him. I'd had a major intellectual crush on him ever since I had discovered his writings while at Cambridge. I had devoured his book *The Pendulum Years* and would meticulously clip his columns, underline them, and save them in a file (no, I did not put pressed flowers in the file, but I might as well have). So when I found out that he was on the panel, I was reduced to an inarticulate bundle of fear. I'm still amazed that in my fog I actually managed to recognize Schumann's Fourth Symphony.

At the end of the taping, he asked me out to dinner for the following week. All I remember is that I spent the week in a state of high anxiety, prepping, primping, and getting myself up to date on Northern Ireland, recent developments in the Soviet Union, and the latest Wagner recordings. I had so many fear butterflies during dinner, I basically just rearranged the food on my plate. I must have bored him to death, because he made sure our second date didn't involve a lot of talking. He took me to Covent Garden to see

Wagner's *Mastersingers*. As you might have guessed by now, I spent the time between the dinner and the opera date reading all about *Mastersingers*—and considering more has been written about Wagner than anyone else except Jesus Christ, that meant a lot of reading.

That week we started a relationship that would last until the end of 1980, when I left London to move to New York. In many ways Bernard was, in fact, the reason I left London. I was thirty by then and still deeply in love with him, but I longed to have children. He, on the other hand, never wanted to have children or get married. What was touching about him was that he saw this rejection not as a badge of independence and freedom for me but as a character flaw in him, a by-product of his deepest fears. He even wrote about it. And the fear he described is by no means confined to men: "What fear of revealing, of vulnerability, of being human, grips us so fiercely, and above all why? What is it that, down there in the darkness of the psyche, cries its silent 'No' to the longing for 'Yes'?" For him this "No" often coincided with a retreat into depression—which he described as "that dark lair where the sick soul's desire for solitude turns into misanthropy." No wonder he loved cats so much. "Above all," he wrote once, "I love the detachment of cats, their willingness to be loved but not to respond beyond a certain, very clearly defined point; no cat ever gave its entire heart to any human being."

I have since talked with dozens of women trapped in relationships like mine, in which the man is not able or willing to match our longing for a deeper intimacy. And however necessary it is, it's incredibly hard and painful to extricate ourselves. Instead we keep trying to make things better—by which we mean make *ourselves* better. I know how hard I worked to gain Bernard's approval. Because on some level I feared that I had fallen short—that if it weren't for *my* shortcomings, we would be spending our lives together. Rationally I knew that his intimacy and commitment issues were *his* and had little or nothing to do with me, but irrationally I feared that it was I who wasn't enough. And in the process I stayed long after it was clear that I was no longer being true to myself.

In fact, I still marvel at what reserves of fearlessness I must have tapped into to be able to leave him. And not just to leave him—the first big love of my life, as well as a mentor as a writer and a role model as a thinker—but also to leave London and to change continents. But I had to. Our lives in London were so inextricably intertwined that I couldn't live there any longer. A quarter of a century later, I can still feel how painful that decision was.

WHAT I LEARNED

Our mistakes can be blessings from which we discover a lot about ourselves. The only thing that matters is not to repeat the same mistakes—but to make fresh ones all the time!

SUZYN WALDMAN

New York Yankees Radio Broadcaster

The year 1987, my first in sports broadcasting, was not an easy one. I was new in the Yankees clubhouse. I was extremely nervous and aware that game after game the male reporters were waiting for me to make a mistake.

I rarely asked a player a question when another reporter was in the vicinity. One evening, Yankees outfielder Dave Winfield had a particularly great game. I mustered up all my courage, and with my tape recorder going, I started to ask my question—and made a mistake with his stats. Two things ran through my mind. *Do I keep going, pretend I didn't notice, and not be able to use the tape, or do I stop the tape and make it clear to everyone here that I made a mistake?* Dave Winfield made the decision for me. He put his hand on the machine's Stop button, knowing I had reversed the stats, and said, "I don't like the way I started to answer that. Can we do it again?" My mistake had led to an incredible act of kindness by a relative stranger.

Not long after that incident, I was on the radio with a local talk show host. He was badgering me about a certain player, and not wanting to appear uninformed, I got the statistics and the details of a game wrong. My error was fodder for a media critic in New York City, giving him another reason to write that women don't know anything about sports and shouldn't be on the air. A friend of mine said, "Oh, forget it. You just made a mistake!"

WHAT I LEARNED

I wasn't prepared. I promised myself that would never happen again. "Be prepared" was a life lesson I should have learned from Dave Winfield in the Yankees clubhouse, but didn't. This time, instead of saying to myself that everyone makes mistakes, I focused on why it happened. From that day forward, I never went on the air unprepared. And if I don't know the answer to a question now, I am not afraid to say a simple "I don't know. I'll find out!"

PETE HAMILL

Author

Looking back, the dumbest thing I ever did was also the most crucial thing to the man I later became.

In the summer of 1951, when I was sixteen, I dropped out of high school at the end of my sophomore year. The reasons were complicated. I was the oldest son of Irish immigrants, living in a blue-collar neighborhood of Brooklyn. My parents worked very hard, but there was never enough money for a family that would soon include seven children. As the oldest son, I wanted desperately to help ease their burden through the only possible way known to people like us: work.

At the time, I was a scholarship student at a splendidly rigorous school called Regis, run by the Jesuits on Eighty-fourth Street off Park Avenue. Each morning, I rose in our Brooklyn tenement and took three subway lines to my destination on the Upper East Side. Then (and now), that part of the world was as different from mine as any two places could be under the same American flag. That world of imperious apartment houses (guarded by uniformed doormen), of aloof white sandstone mansions, of nannies wheeling small children, of the heavy thump of limousine doors during morning pickups, of trees that blossomed each spring, seemed to a Brooklyn boy to be held together by one pervasive attitude. That attitude was about certainty. They were the city's winners, owners of the metropolis, and they would rule forever. They were absolutely free of uncertainty or doubt. Or so I then thought.

At the same time, my own doubts and uncertainties were seething in my brain. What was to become of me? What could I ever do in this life? At Regis, I labored over Caesar's *Gallic War*, but nobody I ever met could speak Latin, not even priests (who merely recited it at mass). At the same time, like most teenagers, I was in hormone overload and wanted desperately to commit sins of the flesh. But how could I ever use Latin to achieve that goal? What Brooklyn girl would ever know Latin? And I wanted many other things I could never get. For example, to have my father hug me (a human gesture, I learned later, that was very rare among the Irish). I wanted to see the world that I'd read about in books: the cities of North Africa, the glories of Rome and Paris and Dublin, the islands of the Pacific, the coasts of Asia. I wanted everything out there, beyond the streets of Brooklyn.

I could draw and began to imagine a life as a cartoonist. My heroes were Milton Caniff, who wrote and drew *Terry and the Pirates* and later *Steve Canyon;* Roy Crane, who did *Buz Sawyer;* Will Eisner of *The Spirit;* and Hal Foster, the master of *Prince Valiant*. I kept reading the comics in the daily newspapers (there were eight New York papers then) and admiring other cartoonists, above all the work of Willard Mullin, the sports cartoonist for the *World-Telegram and Sun*. Of what use was Latin to do such work? Or worse, algebra?

I was also a boy of my times. I didn't know a single person in my neighborhood who had gone to a university. The young men from the neighborhood who had fought (and survived) World War II came home to the immense gift of the GI Bill of Rights. As far as I know, none of them used the educational benefits. They married the girls they'd left behind and took advantage of low-interest VA mortgages to move to the green glades of the suburbs. I thought, without much conviction, *If I drop out, I can always go on to art school. But I must put high school behind me.*

And so I did.

Almost immediately I felt stabs of anguish. My mother, who had accomplished the impossible back in Belfast by graduating from high school, tried to persuade me to change my mind. She failed, and seemed to sag with her failure—and mine. My father, who had gone only to the eighth grade, was more a prisoner of what I later called "the green ceiling." That state of mind was pervasive among Irish people (and other immigrants, of course) who had come through the rigors of immigration and the Great Depression. To such people, certain ambitions were evidence of the sin of pride. And if not seen as sin, vaulting ambition was viewed as absolutely unrealistic. They felt the deck was stacked against the Irish, and they did not want their children to desire things that would only end up in rejection or hurt. Better to take the test for the cops or the fire department. Even better, they should look for a federal civil service job. That would be the best defense against another depression.

That summer of 1951, I found what seemed to be a perfect job: I took the test for an opening at the Brooklyn Navy Yard as an apprentice sheet metal worker. I passed. By September, I was working as a young "tin knocker" at the yard, in the company of men, including at least one cousin. I was set, my father said, for the next thirty years. Depression or no depression. I was part of the federal civil service.

But the anguish did not go away. Distant shores kept whispering to me. If I could not see them, perhaps I could draw them. I started taking a drawing course at night in the Cartoonists and Illustrators School in Manhattan, under the direction of Burne Hogarth, the artist of *Tarzan*. I would arrive at the school around six, exhausted by work at the Navy Yard, nap in the lobby, start class at seven, and begin working on my emerging vision of a possible life. For the first time, I was among young people who had a sense of the future. They would go on to study in Paris or Rome. Or they would work for Will Eisner and then create their own strips. They listened to Hogarth, who told us: "The stages of an artist's development are simple: imitate, emulate, equal, and surpass." They were all certain that they would surpass.

I started forming a new plan. Things were getting slightly better at home, thanks to my father's union. So I would join the navy itself, get a high school equivalency diploma, then use the GI Bill to go on to art school. I would sail across the Pacific and go to Korea, where a bitter war was being fought. I would escape Brooklyn. At some point that year, I saw *An American in Paris,* and there was Gene Kelly playing a guy named Mulligan, a Mick like me, singing, dancing, and painting in Paris. And he had Leslie Caron too. In September 1952, I joined the U.S. Navy. The Korean War came to an end in the spring of 1953, and I ended up at the naval air station in Pensacola, read Hemingway and Fitzgerald and Dos Passos for the first time at the excellent base library, and finally met people who had been to university. If they could do it, so could I. Every one of them urged me on. "You only have one life, man," one said. And the two of us listened to Hank Williams on the jukebox.

From there I went on to live my life: art school in Mexico in 1956 (even then I couldn't afford Paris on the $110 a month from the GI Bill), graphic arts work in New York, finally the newspaper business. Along the way, I gave up cartooning for painting and failed out of painting (in my own eyes) into writing.

But I had also developed the habit of continually making up for the mistake of dropping out of high school. In the company of friends, I read the classics (my copy of Aristotle's *Ethics* was full of my underlinings of the wrong passages). I absorbed the newest work. I moved around with Camus in my head and Sartre, and also Kerouac and Burroughs and Corso. Joyce moved into my skull to stay, and one writer always led to another. As a reporter, I learned about my own city on the streets, but also absorbed the city's history, the dense, thrilling narrative that had preceded my arrival. I lived as a reporter in Barcelona and Dublin, San Juan and Rome, and visited many other places, from Saigon to Belfast to Managua. With the exceptions of Dublin and Belfast (which felt like home), I moved through these places as a New Yorker. They all taught me something about my own city. I also learned Spanish, an experience that taught me about my own language.

What I Learned

I learned that education only could end with death. Now I realize that I've been playing catch-up ball since I was sixteen. Even now, playing in overtime, I wake up wanting to know something new, whether the instructor is the *New York Times* or Cicero. Every writer is an autodidact at heart, of course, and I am no exception. I have an ongoing project now: reading again those books I thought I had read when young. From *Don Quixote* to *Bleak House,* they are now books filled with human riches, because between readings I have lived my life, for better or worse. Now I know much about human folly (including my own) and human grandeur, about decency and evil. A few years ago, I even reread Caesar's *Gallic War,* the grinding curse of my adolescence. This time around, the book was a joy. It was a model of clarity, its prose filled with rhythms that I realized had been engraved in my own mind for life. I wanted to thank someone, but the poor Jesuit who tried to help me to accept his gifts is almost certainly dead. These words will have to do. Yes: Gaul is divided into three parts. Just like many human lives.

JULIAN SCHLOSSBERG

Motion Picture, Theater, and Television Producer

During the early 1960s, I had just graduated from college and had already served in the army. A college friend, older than I was, worked for an employment agency. He knew I wanted to get into show business and told me of a job at the NBC television network. It turned out the work was in Englewood, New Jersey, right over the George Washington Bridge.

I went to the office of the supervisor and was asked a lot of questions about my background. The interview seemed to be going very well when he asked what my immediate goal was. With a smile I said, "To have *your* job." He just stared at me. "Only kidding," I added quickly, with what I thought was a warm smile. The interview came to an end and we shook hands and said our goodbyes.

As soon as I returned to New York City, my friend at the employment agency called and told me that I had been too aggressive in the interview. Obviously, I didn't get the job.

WHAT I LEARNED

Kenny Rogers's song "The Gambler" has the most apropos lyric: "You gotta know when to hold 'em, know when to fold 'em." As any good performer can tell you: know your audience.

PHIL KEOGHAN

Host of *The Amazing Race*

At nineteen, I thought nothing could hurt me. I felt invincible and had no understanding of how fragile life was. I thought nothing of risking my life, flirting with disaster, always assuming that somehow I was different from everyone else. Sure, I had a few close calls, but nothing woke me up until I found myself lost underwater inside a 22,000-ton shipwreck, running out of air.

I got my first hosting job on an adventure television show when I was nineteen, in New Zealand. There were three hosts and every week people would write in and get us to do things they'd like to see on TV. One of my first assignments was to go with a team of divers and a camera crew down into a sunken ship. The vessel had never been filmed before and was filled with some great stuff. Although I was a pretty inexperienced diver at the time and very claustrophobic, I couldn't wait to go.

I followed another diver into the water, and he kept going down, down, down, until we came to this massive cruise ship lying on its side. Right away, the other diver slipped through a porthole and into the ship, and I followed him through liquid corridors and dark passageways. Everything was covered in silt. We navigated this underwater maze and ended up swimming into a former ballroom where everything, including swaying chandeliers, was preserved almost perfectly underwater.

At first it was a dreamlike experience, but it soon turned into a nightmare. Somehow we got separated from the camera crew. So we were hanging around in this underwater ballroom with our lights off to save battery power. And suddenly my dive buddy turned his light on. He signaled to me, "Stay put!" and then just like that he was gone. So now I was alone, deep inside a mass of steel. It was pitch-dark and dead quiet, and I didn't know where up and down were. I started to panic.

I was thinking, *Where did this guy go? What if he doesn't come back?* I started checking my air gauge and then beating the valve, which meant I was breathing so fast that I started taking in water. I panicked to find my light and turn it back on. Claustrophobia took over as I realized I was lost inside a mass of steel and was running out of air. I was wondering if I should stay put or try to swim out, knowing that if I moved they'd never find me if they did come back. I briefly managed to be rational, and then lost it—every minute my fear grew. My life started flashing in front of me. But I was not thinking about what I'd done—instead, I was thinking about all the things I hadn't done. There was so much I wanted to do with my life, and now I'd never get the chance. What an idiot I'd been. How could I have been so stupid?

What I Learned

Well, obviously I did get out of that nightmare. My buddy came back. When he finally got me back to the dive boat, I realized my life had changed forever. I couldn't wait to start living. I couldn't wait to write a list. The only piece of paper I could find was a paper bag, and I just started dumping down everything I felt I needed to do with my life. I made a contract with myself to seize the day and live without regret. Now, bear in mind that I was nineteen, a young man, so obviously there are some things I'm not going to tell you about . . . *But* the first thing was to go back into the shipwreck, get back on the horse and face that fear. Ever since my biggest mistake, I've had a list on which I keep ticking off, adding, deleting . . . I move things around, and that helps keep me focused on living the biggest possible life I can. This is where my philosophy "No Opportunity Wasted," or "NOW," comes from.

I decided that the best life I could have would be to turn my list into a career, to get paid to do all the things I had on my list. And after a lot of hard work, that's exactly what happened. Prior to working on *The Amazing Race*, I traveled to more than sixty countries making other television shows like *Keoghan's Heroes* and *Phil Keoghan's Adventure Crazy*, doing everything from swimming from Asia to Europe across the Bosporus, to lugging a three-hundred-pound chef to the top of an erupting volcano for a five-star dinner.

Now, you might say, *Clearly he didn't learn a lesson from his experience in the shipwreck. He's still risking his life.* Well, no: I've learned my lesson. I'm more careful about how I do things. I no longer leap without looking or just forge ahead without a thorough plan. I no longer take life for granted; I treat it with respect. Life really is a gift, a gift that comes with an expiration date, and it is up to all of us to make the most of it!

GIL SCHWARTZ

Author

There are all kinds of mistakes: little ones that slip off your back like water from the feathers of an arctic gull, midsize errors that seem to disappear for a while, then pop up like a mole from an unexpected hole in the tundra of everyday life, big ones that make you stop for a moment and wonder where all those precious brain cells you were once so proud of might have gone.

And then there are the mistakes that are more than simple missteps of one size or another: acts that in themselves reveal yawning flaws in your character and make you wish that time in its haste would stand still, turn, and give you that one critical moment back, things that cannot be erased, spun, cleansed of their base matter, that can only be learned from. Knowledge gathered does not erase the mistake, for in its essence it is something done that cannot be undone. Hopefully, however, some insights may be gained, some sour, bitter slice of wisdom that, in future, can be drawn on to minimize the chances that one may stray so far from the light again.

When I was thirty-one, my father was admitted to the hospital with the symptoms of a stroke. He was sixty-five and had been of middling health for a while. It turned out, after extensive testing, not to be a stroke precisely, but rather to be a related circulatory problem that led to similar symptoms. He wasn't himself, though. He seemed smaller in the hospital bed than I had ever seen him, and while he had received certain assurances from the doctors that things were not at a critical point, he was frightened. My father was an atheist to the bone, not even a cowardly agnostic, and the prospect of the utter void that, as far as he was concerned, followed our stay on this earth yawned very large indeed to him.

My father and I were not on the best of terms, hadn't been for years. There were a lot of excellent reasons for each of us, and fault enough to go around, I see now, on both sides. The tension between us was particularly painful for him and for me because when I was a child we were uncommonly close. And even after the permafrost descended after I married, I still doubted that he adored me with the fierce, profound merging of identities that distinguishes a truly great neurotic love from its more comfortable and managed counterpart. Ah, how he loved his little boy! And when that boy became a man, how he missed that little fellow, and how sad I was in my heart that I could not give him that gift of perpetual infantile devotion.

Still, after a period of horrendous discomfort, we settled into an almost equally terrifying cordiality that was somewhat better. And there we stayed, drifting like two ships in a giant sea of love, blame, memory, and regret, just keeping each other in sight but never drawing close enough to engage in any meaningful way with each other. Years went by. Nothing changed, but then, nothing got worse either. And then there he was, suddenly, in that sad little hospital gown, looking at me from his cranked-up bed, hair askew, eyes filled with fear and hurt and anger, for above all my dad was an extremely proud guy who really resented being in this ignoble position.

I was telling him, that night, about how my wife and I were going to take a few days upstate over the weekend. This was a long-scheduled trip. I didn't really want to go. I had a bad feeling about it. But it was, you know, something we had wanted to do. And why not? The doctors said that everything was probably going to be just fine. There had been some surgery. It had gone pretty well. My dad was going to be released pending the results of a few more tests.

"We'll be back Sunday night," I told him. He kind of glared at me. "Well," he said, "I guess I must be doing better than I thought."

I told him I loved him, gave him a kiss on his stubbly cheek, and got out of there, feeling like a felon leaving the scene of a crime, which, I suppose, I was, although the crime in question is not one that is written in any temporal book. Nonetheless, it's real. I'm guilty of it. My sentence for it will never be commuted.

That night up in the Catskills somewhere, I could not sleep. I was hot, then cold. Bugs zoomed around my ear. There were way too many crickets. After a while, it started to rain, big, heavy drops that sounded like hailstones on the thin roof of the cottage our friends had loaned us for our getaway. Thunder followed, walking across the sky with great, heavy boots, accompanied by rippling blasts of lightning. In the darkened house, as my wife slept, I rose and paced the strange rooms with a mounting sensation that everything was wrong. Everything. And as that maelstrom raged both inside me and in the world outside and above, I felt my father's spirit reach out to me across those ninety miles and say to me, as if I heard it in my ear, "Come to me. Please come to me now." And yet I did not come.

At six a.m. the telephone rang. I had given the number to my mother in case of emergency. I don't need to tell you what she told me. My dad lived for another week or so, but he never woke up. I sat by his bedside holding his hand, which didn't feel like his hand at all. It was cold and slightly puffy, where before it had been dry and firm and warm. Not his hand. Not his face either, because the eyes are the windows of the soul, as you know, and his were empty, so empty. I spoke to him, of course. Told him how much I loved him, how much I regretted not being with him when he needed me, how much I regretted all the time we had wasted fighting with each other. He didn't answer. They tell you that people at the end do hear you, even if it appears they do not. I hope he did hear me. I tell myself that he did, because it makes me feel better, but not really.

When my mom died last summer, nearly twenty-five years after losing the love of her life, I was sitting next to her on the bed, holding her tiny, frail hand in both of mine. I have never felt more clearly that I was in a place where I was meant to be. So maybe I learned a little something between these two great and terrible passings.

What I Learned

Certain events in your life present you with a choice for which you get one chance and one chance only to do what should be done. We must seize those moments and hold them close, no matter how difficult they may be, for they are the stuff of which destiny is made.

SALLY KELLERMAN

Actress (Hot Lips, *M*A*S*H*)

When I was a kid I was a huge fan of Bing Crosby and Danny Kaye.

Then maybe at the beginning of junior high, I went to see *Viva Zapata!* and my life changed. Marlon Brando was so thrilling and sexy and gorgeous.

With Jean Peters lying in bed in the background, Marlon stood looking out the window wearing only these white Mexican drawstring pajama bottoms. It's an image I'll never forget.

I saw every movie he did. I must have seen *The Men* at least four or five times and *The Wild One* seven times, and later when I was out of high school I saw *Guys and Dolls* seven times.

I always felt so chubby and unattractive, and I thought Marlon would understand me, because I read once that he had struggled with weight, even though he was so skinny and gorgeous in all these movies.

I was hanging out with my best friend, Luana Anders. Luana starred in Francis Ford Coppola's first film, *Dementia 13*, and later she was in *Easy Rider*.

Luana and I were in *Reform School Girl*. She was the star and I was a bit player. I wasn't exactly making a living in show business at this time.

One day, I was driving down Hollywood Boulevard and I looked over to see this old white car, and who was driving but Marlon Brando. I thought, *Oh, no—that can't possibly be him, because that's an old beat-up car.* I had the idea that a movie star would be driving a big fancy one. But it was him, and oh my God I was over the moon.

Another night I went to the movies. It was pouring down rain. I got out of my car, looked over, and saw Marlon going into the theater. I don't remember the movie. All I could think of was that I was in the same theater with Marlon Brando. When the movie was over I looked for him, and I thought I saw him, but I wasn't sure.

One day I told Luana, "I think I'm going to see Marlon tonight," and she said, "Oh, don't say that—you're scaring me, because you probably are." Sure enough, I went to a restaurant that I had never been to. I don't remember who took me there. It was a fancy restaurant with red booths. And there he was, sitting at a table with some people. It was more than I could bear. My heart nearly fell out of my chest.

Another night I went to Cosmo Alley because Stan Getz was playing and because I knew that Marlon's friend Carlo Fiore was the bouncer. I knew Carlo. He was sweet to me, a nice friend. Again, I forget who brought me there, but we walked into the music part of the club, and there was Marlon. Carlo introduced me to him and sat me down beside him. I weighed about 175 pounds and was five foot ten, with short bleached blond hair. Here I was with my big fat face, talking a hundred miles a minute. Marlon was famous for liking quiet Asian and black girls, so I was anything but his type. When the music was over, I didn't move. He didn't move. My friend said, "Sally, I'm leaving now." Without looking I said, "Okay, goodbye." Pretty soon Marlon looked over at me and said with a smirk, "All right, so what are you—an actress?" To which I responded, "Yes, I am, and I don't think it's funny," and he said, "Well, would you like to go for a ride?" I said, "Yes, I would."

We went to his car and got in and drove around the block. He went to put his arm around me, and I said, "What are you doing?" He said, "Right. I wouldn't want to spoil this beautiful friendship." He turned the car around and dropped me off. I was a virgin. I could never have slept with him. I was just excited to have a little ride with him. I could hardly wait to tell my pal Luana.

There were a couple of other nights I went back to Cosmo Alley and would be sitting there with Marlon and some different people. He was always asking questions: "How old are you, Sally?" "Do you have a boyfriend?" All these questions—I didn't know what they were because I was so stunned to be in his presence. I was never myself around him.

I pined away for two years after that, trying to get over my crush on Marlon, while I was working as a waitress in a place called Chez Paulette up on the Sunset Strip. It was a hangout for people like Steve McQueen, Warren Beatty, John Cassavetes, and friends like Jack Nicholson, James Coburn, and Robert Blake, and all kinds of producers and directors. I was in heaven.

One night after closing I was wiping off the tables and I looked up and saw Marlon coming in with this tall blond guy. This was around the time he was shooting *The Young Lions*. They sat down at the other end of the restaurant, and I went on cleaning tables, but my heart had stopped. I went over and said, "Here are your menus." I didn't say hello or anything and walked away. When I came back I said, as coolly as I could, "May I take your order?" I took the order and went back to cleaning tables.

It was a small coffeehouse, and I was staying as far away from them as I could. I finally had to do tables closer to where they were sitting. I was doing everything with my back to them. Suddenly, I heard this voice say, "Sally, don't you remember me, or are you playing it cool?" I whirled around and blurted out, "I'm playing it cool, because every minute I've ever spent with you was the worst minute of my whole life." He smiled at me and said, "Would you like to come up to the house?" "Yes, I would." We got in the car with the blond man, and I was like a wooden Indian the whole way up to his house—just so scared and excited. We got up there, and Marlon had to go to the bathroom, so he leaped out of the car and ran into his house, and the blond guy said to me, "It must be wonderful to be so quiet and calm."

We went inside and wound up sitting on Marlon's bed—the three of us. I forget much of the conversation, but all I remember is that I said something, and Marlon, being sympathetic, reached over and touched my leg.

I said, "Don't touch me, because you'll never touch me as much as I want you to." I got weepy, and the next thing you know this blond guy was gone and I was alone in the room with Marlon.

Either I looked good or my crying appealed to him, because I knew I was not his type. I spent the whole night in his bed, fending him off because I wanted to be special. He was so mad at me. The next morning he had to get up to go to a meeting, and I said, "Well, you can't be mad at me because I didn't sleep with you!" Oy.

What I Learned

I was a putz. If a similar opportunity affords itself in my next life—I'm there.

JONATHAN ALTER

Senior Editor, *Newsweek* Magazine

Considering the thousands of articles I've written over a twenty-five-year career as a journalist, I've been lucky: plenty of little errors but no libel suits or big screwups. There is, however, one column I'd very much like to have back—a column that to this day makes me wince at the thought of it. This column was not technically inaccurate, but it was still a mistake—a big mistake—to write it. It was published in *Newsweek* in late 2001 under the headline "Time to Think About Torture."

The column began: "In this autumn of anger, even a liberal can find his thoughts turning to . . . torture." After explaining that no suspects were talking in the investigation into the greatest crime in American history (9/11), the story suggested psychological torture (loud music, sleep deprivation), truth serum, and deportation to less squeamish allies as things to consider to crack the case. I went through how Israel handled terror suspects, the problems of what to do in the so-called ticking time bomb hypothetical (in which a terrorist in custody knows about a bomb but won't talk), and explained that torture does sometimes work. The column concluded with the thought that "we can't legalize physical torture. It's contrary to American values," but we needed to think about psychological interrogation and letting tough allies do some of the dirty work. The final sentence read: "Nobody said this was going to be pretty."

After the column came out, the *New York Times* ran an article about how liberals were reconciling themselves to torture and used my piece as Exhibit A. The fact that I was not advocating physical torture was, of course, lost in the translation. For a time, I clung to this as an excuse. I rationalized that it wasn't my fault if people ignored my distinction between physical and psychological torture.

We now know that late 2001 was exactly the period when the Pentagon loosened its restrictions on torture, disregarded the Geneva Conventions, and began a policy (also used occasionally during the Clinton administration) of "extraordinary rendition"—deporting terror suspects to be tortured elsewhere. I have no evidence that my column contributed in even a small way to making it easier for the Bush administration to pursue these new policies. But I do know that such policies have been proven wrong morally and are harmful to the war on terrorism.

I've now read enough about torture to know that it simply does not work in obtaining credible information from suspects (the stories saying it did have been largely discredited). Tortured suspects talk, but they almost never say anything useful. Worse, by winking at torture, the United States has not just violated important international agreements but turned its back on its own most sacred principles. In purely practical terms, torture at Abu Ghraib, Guantánamo Bay, and other American prisons have made it much harder for the United States to set a humanitarian tone and push for global democracy. At a deeper level, sanctioning torture undermines who we are as a people. Many Americans understood this even in the angry aftermath of September 11. I just wish I had been one of them.

WHAT I LEARNED

When you're angry about something, whether personal or political, make sure that emotions don't overwhelm reason. There are times to be intentionally provocative, but not when the result may contribute to hurting people unnecessarily. On sensitive issues, trying to protect oneself with caveats and rhetorical loopholes is foolhardy. Only the larger point comes through, and you are responsible for foreseeing that. Finally, we need to think like terrorists to help figure out where they might strike next, but not to act like them.

SUSAN UNGARO

President, James Beard Foundation, and Former Editor in Chief, *Family Circle* Magazine

It was the New York media trial of 2002. Rosie O'Donnell had shut down her new magazine and the company for which I worked, Gruner & Jahr USA, was suing the television talk show host. I was caught in the middle of the fight, because I had helped her start her magazine, *Rosie*. At the time, I was the editor in chief of *Family Circle*, which was also owned by G&J USA. The company asked me to also serve as editorial consultant on the launch of Rosie's magazine. Things had not gone smoothly, to say the least. I and others ended up being caught in the middle. And so I found myself involved in daylong depositions and pre-trial pressures of being the lead witness on the opening day of the trial. My view of the much-publicized breakup was that both sides had made mistakes, so I was not being viewed all that favorably by my company. Clearly that made me nervous.

The night before the trial, my husband, Colin, was traveling on business and our eight-year-old daughter, Christina, didn't want to go to sleep. It was past nine-thirty and I felt I needed to reread the 300-plus pages of my deposition before morning. (I had heard that the one thing you don't want to do on the witness stand is contradict your testimony.) When Christina got out of bed for the third or fourth time, I snapped and crankily told her she had to go to sleep because Mommy had a big day tomorrow in court.

"What's the matter?" she asked.

I showed her the two-inch-thick binder and said I had to read all of it tonight because I was going to court before a judge tomorrow. "And I don't want to make any mistakes," I added.

She replied, "Don't you know, Mommy, all you have to do is tell the truth and you won't go to jail."

Her innocent but right-as-rain reply made me smile in spite of my tension. All of a sudden I realized I didn't have to study my deposition, because I had simply told it like it was. All the office politics had blurred my sense of right and wrong. And so . . . I closed the deposition, took her into her bedroom, lay down beside her, and got a good night's sleep.

WHAT I LEARNED

My mother always said, "There are three sides to every story: his, hers, and the truth." It used to bug my brothers and me when we were fighting for Mom to take our side. Yet I had found myself repeating my mother's words when my three children had quarreled, trying to get my husband or me to take sides. It took my young daughter's innocent sense of justice to remind me that despite the flurry and stress of office politics, business scandals, and even high courtroom drama, the only true source of being at peace with yourself is to remain true to your values and simply tell the truth (even if it sometimes hurts).

MIKHAIL BARYSHNIKOV

Impresario, Dancer, Director

Well, I've made a million mistakes that surprisingly didn't affect my life on a big scale, but I think the most regrettable moments come from when I've been in a position to influence and haven't extended my arm to someone I felt needed help. It wasn't always clear what that person needed, but it bothers me that maybe I didn't do the right thing at the right time.

WHAT I LEARNED

I should look more closely into what's in people's eyes and try to respond better.

WALTER CRONKITE

CBS Anchorman

My biggest mistake was retiring from the anchorman's chair at the *CBS Evening News*. In taking that fateful step I was living up to a yearlong resolve that I would retire on my sixty-fifth birthday to enjoy some of the still reasonably certain active years with my children and grandchildren—on the sailboat and the tennis court. I'd take them and my dear wife, Betsy, to the many exotic lands I'd had the privilege of visiting as a foreign correspondent.

WHAT I LEARNED

Had I known I was going to live this long, I might not have stepped down from the anchor desk so soon and missed out on a lot of the dandy stories of this last quarter century. However, I would not change the opportunities and the fun I've had with my family and friends, and the folks I've met sailing and traveling in these ensuing years.

KATHIE LEE GIFFORD

Entertainer, Playwright

I love you too much to deny you the *privilege* of making mistakes."

Sounds funny at first, doesn't it? But that's exactly what my daddy used to tell me when I was growing up.

Well, I'm still "growing up" and I'm still making mistakes, and I'm still remembering my daddy and all the wisdom he imparted to me. I'm grateful every day that I had a father who understood how valuable mistakes can be. Because although I've had my share of success and good fortune, it has been my mistakes that have taught me the most.

I think the thing that has surprised me is that a mistake is a dynamic thing. Like any action, there is always a reaction. There are always consequences.

I don't think we realize that when we're young we make decisions that have the power to have an impact on the rest of our lives.

For me that was the decision to give up piano lessons after four years of study. I had adored music since my earliest memory and dreamed of someday having a career in the entertainment business. But as a young teenager—and therefore a *genius who knows everything*—I decided that cheerleading was far more important to my development as a human being. (I'm embarrassed to admit this even today.)

Anyway, it doesn't take much effort to surmise that I haven't led a cheer or done a cartwheel, a C-jump, or a split in a very long time, but I have been a professional musician for forty years. Not having the skills that come from having a solid command of a musical instrument has made a difficult career choice even more difficult— not impossible, but far more difficult.

I watch other people sit down at a piano and effortlessly play sonatas or concertos or ragtime or swing or folk or rock and roll or even a little ditty and I've got to admit I regret my decision so many years ago. And it's not even all about *performance*. It's about the simple joy of being able to create beauty anytime one wants to, in the privacy of one's own imagination.

I cheated myself out of a blessing and I have no one to blame but myself.

My daddy also used to say, "Honey, find something you love to do and then figure out a way to get paid for it." He understood that where your true passion is, there your joy is also. And a joyful life is a truly successful life. Perhaps not by the world's standards, but whose life is it, anyway?

I'm grateful I was able to take steps later in my life that ensured I could continue in a business I loved. I majored in voice in college. I have continued with voice lessons ever since. And after I left *Live with Regis and Kathie Lee,* I began a whole new career as a songwriter and playwright that I never dreamed I was capable of.

But my daddy knew.

Years ago he was tape-recording me singing a simple little childhood song a cappella. I must have been about five years old. After singing a phrase or two I looked around, surprised that there was no musical accompaniment.

"Where's da moosic, Daddy?" I asked.

"Oh, sweetheart," I can still remember him tenderly saying, "you've got to learn to make your own music."

What I Learned

Make no mistake, it's never too late to start.

LEONARD NIMOY

Actor (Mr. Spock, *Star Trek*)

Having established a relationship with a California company that had published two books of my poetry, I agreed that we would develop a sort of *Star Trek* memoir. The book was to deal with questions that I was frequently being asked: "How did you get the role of Spock?" "What was your favorite episode?" "How did you prepare for the character?" and so on. This was at the time when an intense interest in *Star Trek* was building as a result of a very successful syndication of the original series.

During the writing process I had an experience at the San Francisco airport that prompted an idea for a chapter in the book. A lady with a young child in tow recognized me. She stood with the boy, perhaps nine or ten years old, in front of me and announced to him, "This is your favorite character on television. This is Mr. Spock." The child looked at me with a blank stare, obviously confused by the information his mother had given him. For him this was not Mr. Spock standing in front of him: no pointed ears, no arched eyebrows, no greenish skin, and no *Star Trek* uniform. Of course, what the mother meant was "This is the actor who plays Mr. Spock," but that's not what she said.

As a result of the confrontation I wrote a chapter titled "I Am Not Spock." I told about the differences between the character and myself. My parents were immigrants from Russia. Spock's certainly were not. My parents were both humans. Spock was born of a

Vulcan father and a human mother. I enumerated the differences and then went on to explain how the character was built.

When the book was finished I had a discussion with the publishers about potential titles. I suggested that the title of the chapter "I Am Not Spock" might be provocative and engender interest as the title of the book. The publisher warned me that it was a negative title and that negative titles tended not to sell well. I gave him a wise-guy response. I said, "What about *Gone with the Wind*?" He said, "Very well; the book is yours. We'll title it whatever you want," and that's the way it went out.

At the time there was enormous hunger for more *Star Trek* but there were no episodes being produced. When the book was published the very intense *Star Trek* audience came to believe, as a result of that title, that I was rejecting the character and all things connected with *Star Trek*. The widely held belief was that my position was preventing more *Star Trek* from being produced. None of this was true. In fact, in the book I took pains to comment on my deep caring for the character and for what he and *Star Trek* offered. Nevertheless, the rumors persisted, and many more people read the title than read the book. Using the title *I Am Not Spock* was a big mistake.

In 1977 George Lucas's *Star Wars* opened to enormous audiences. Paramount Pictures, the holders of the *Star Trek* franchise, took note and we went into production on the first of several *Star Trek* movies, which were followed by subsequent *Star Trek* TV series. The rumors subsided, and I was welcomed back into the *Star Trek* fold.

What I Learned

Today, I am still not convinced that negative titles are a problem. The current *Fiasco* and *State of Denial*, though quite negative in name and content, are selling briskly. Nevertheless, if I had it to do again, I would give more thought to my publisher's concern rather than simply brushing it aside with my wise-guy response.

Live and learn.

ISADORE ROSENFELD, MD

Rossi Distinguished Professor of Clinical Medicine, Weill Cornell Medical Center

The Albert Lasker Medical Research Award jury was set up by the late Mary Lasker, whom I always considered to be the American equivalent of Florence Nightingale because of her belief in the importance of medical research. For many years, she successfully lobbied every American president from Richard Nixon to George H. W. Bush for their commitment to medical research. The jury was composed of leading scientists and researchers in various fields of medicine and was chaired for many years by Dr. Michael DeBakey. Mary was good enough to appoint me to the jury because I was her personal physician. To this day, most of the winners of the Lasker Award go on to receive the Nobel Prize. In fact, a representative of the Nobel committee often sits on the Lasker jury.

Jury members spend many hours each year reviewing the current literature and considering the scientific contributions of hundreds of researchers worldwide. In 1974, one name came up that appealed to many of the jurors—John Charnley, an English orthopedic surgeon who invented the artificial hip. I did not agree with the nomination. With so many thousands of people dying from heart attacks, strokes, and cancer, I was not in favor of giving this most prestigious award for a mere orthopedic discovery, which at best would provide pain relief for a relatively small number of individuals. I argued in vain. The jury voted to give Charnley the Lasker Award.

Fast-forward to the year 2001. My wife and I were walking at a leisurely pace one morning on Worth Avenue in Palm Beach, Florida. I was suddenly seized by the most severe pain I had ever experienced. My right hip felt as if it had been smashed into pieces; I could barely make it into a cab to return to my hotel a block away. There I needed a wheelchair to get to my room. My wife called an ambulance and I was taken to the emergency room of a local hospital. An X-ray of my hip revealed that it had virtually crumbled. I was flown back to New York the next day, where I underwent immediate hip replacement—thanks to Dr. John Charnley. (The reason my hip fell apart was that many months earlier, while in the Caribbean, I had apparently eaten some fish that contained a toxin that spread throughout my body, affecting my heart, muscles, and nervous system. I recovered fully after receiving large doses of cortisone for several weeks. Unfortunately, in a very small percentage of cases, such steroid therapy can result in bone destruction, notably of the hip. I was fortunate that only one hip was involved.) Today, I can't even tell which one was replaced (but airport security workers can every time I'm screened). Had Charnley not invented the artificial hip, I might well have remained bedridden for the rest of my life. Had my colleagues on the Lasker jury been foolish enough to listen to me and withhold the recognition and prestige that Dr. Charnley deserved, I'd never have forgiven myself. So even with the best of intentions, it's easy to make simple mistakes.

WHAT I LEARNED

In retrospect, the Lasker jury logic was absolutely correct. By 1974, which was when they were considering the award, some 50,000 hip operations were already being performed annually (currently that number is approximately 400,000 a year). The jury estimated—again, correctly—that millions more would ultimately benefit from it.

Note: After my operation, I did some further reading about John

Charnley. He was an extraordinary man. He became interested in bone metabolism early in his career. At one point, he was curious about the role of the thin covering of the bone called the periosteum. Such was his dedication that he actually persuaded a younger colleague to remove a piece of bone from the upper end of his tibia and to implant one piece above and the other beneath the periosteum. I don't know what he learned from that experiment, but he eventually developed osteomyelitis (a severe infection of the bone) of his tibia and required several operations before it was cured. The history of medicine is filled with such examples of unselfishness and devotion to the public good.

DON HEWITT

Creator of *60 Minutes*

My judgment over the years has been pretty good, but it wasn't flawless. I'm the one Barbara Walters came to in the 1950s when she was a producer on the *Today* show and said she'd like to be a broadcaster. "Barbara," I said, "with your voice, no one is going to let you broadcast."

I'm also the guy who told a kid named Marty Ehrlichman back in the early 1960s, when he was working in the CBS film library for maybe sixty dollars a week, to stop coming up with get-rich schemes and pay more attention to his job. One day he came to me and said, "I'm going to quit." "Okay, Marty, now what?" "I'm going to manage a singer." "Oh, shit," I said. "What do you know about managing a singer? What singer?" "Well, I saw her in a club. She's a Jewish girl with a big nose, but she can sing." "Forget it, Marty," I said. "Get rid of her. Get rid of that girl." That girl's name was Barbra Streisand and that kid who worked in the CBS film library for sixty dollars a week got rich and famous by ignoring my advice.

But, for the most part, I seem to have guessed right more than I've guessed wrong. Maybe that's why I'm still around in my eighties and why Senator Tom Daschle of South Dakota, when he toasted Al Newhart, chairman of the Gannett Company and founder of *USA Today,* at his retirement, told the assembled guests that Al had an impossible problem. He was "too old to work for a newspaper and too young to work for *60 Minutes.*"

The truth is that when you've been around as long as I have, you get set in your ways. For example, I am computer illiterate and have no desire to be otherwise. There is nothing I need that I am not willing to go to a store to buy, although I am prepared for the possibility that before too long there may not be any stores (as we know them) or schools (as we know them) or hospitals (as we know them)—that anything we need, from a pair of socks to a college education to medical treatment, will come from a Web site, which is why I got to thinking the other day about what we all took for granted before the computer age. I worked up a scenario in which a man comes home and tells his wife that he heard about a great new gadget that works without any connection to the Internet—no screen, no laptop, no mouse, no gigabytes. A guy named Alexander Graham Bell came up with it. He calls it a telephone, and all you'd have to do is punch in a bunch of numbers that would be listed in something called "a telephone book" and you could talk to anyone in the world—even in Chechnya, if you knew someone there and could find his or her number in the book. Dollars to donuts, his wife would tell him: Oh, God, you're so gullible—you believe anything anyone tells you.

Okay, you say you don't go for Bell's telephone. Try this. I heard about a guy who has invented something called a "post office." There would be one in every town. If you wanted to write a letter to your mother, for thirty-seven cents, a man would personally deliver the letter to her house. How can anyone be as on top of the world as I am and not want to come to terms with the twenty-first century?

WHAT I LEARNED

Maybe liking it "the way it was" gives me a perspective on the way it is, perhaps even the way it will be—or maybe it's just another one of my mistakes.

RON DELSENER

Music Event Producer

Reaching way back, the first mistake I made was when Vivian Miller and her sister, Barbara, gave me a surprise thirteenth birthday party. My sister, Harriette, led me to our "finished" basement at 45-56 193rd Street in Flushing, Queens. There we would play cowboys and Indians or create an ice show in our slippers, sliding on the newly waxed wooden floors. Orchestra seats were folding chairs on the floor, and two chairs on a table were the balcony. A 45 rpm would play Hugo Winterhalter or a Montovani selection while we "skated"! The price of admission was five cents.

Anyway, my sister led me down the stairs and the lights were off. Vivian and Barbara shouted, "Happy birthday!" I was really mad and upset because I did not know what a surprise was. I was (and still am) a "control freak," and reacting to a "surprise" environment that I did not control upset me. I angrily said: "Don't EVER do anything like this again!" Needless to say, they cried. Now, after twenty years of heavy therapy and a stint as a poster boy for every prescription drug, I am happy.

WHAT I LEARNED

If someone upsets you, but you know they were well-meaning, try to be gracious.

CARL REINER

Director, Writer, Actor

I am not sure that there is such a word as *schmuckery*, but if there isn't, I will be happy to contribute it to Messrs. Funk and Wagnall or whoever is in charge of dubious acquisitions for their dictionary's next edition. *Schmuck* is Yiddish slang for "penis" and is used in impolite society to designate someone who does nincompoopy things. For a good part of my life, I have been an active member of that discipline.

I was eighteen years old when I was offered what I consider to be my first well-paying, professional job in the theater. For an eight-week tour of southern colleges and high schools as a member of the Avon Shakespearean Repertory Company, I was to be paid thirty dollars a week!

I traveled by bus to Atlanta, Georgia, the farthest I had ever ventured from my parents' Bronx apartment at 2089 Arthur Avenue. It was the first time I had seen FOR WHITE ONLY and FOR COLORED ONLY signs on drinking fountains and public toilets. I had heard about their existence, but actually seeing the signs and watching people heed them was very unsettling. I encountered many eye-opening and eye-blinking experiences in my eight weeks of traveling through the Deep South, but I will not cite examples of the old South's demeaning and bigoted practices of legal schmuckery. I will instead recall for you a tale of my own personal schmuckery. The passage of the Civil Rights Bill in 1964 helped the South to rid itself of its schmuckerian ways, but I, sad to say, from time to time still struggle with mine.

Our first day of rehearsal for *As You Like It*, being held in the ballroom of the Hotel Tallulah in Atlanta, was most exciting. I had just finished auditioning for the role of Orlando in *As You Like It* and was rather pleased with myself. I didn't quite understand everything I was saying, but I said it all with conviction, a strong voice, and a slight Errol Flynnish English accent. During a break, the managing director of the company, Frank Selman, beckoned me to him. I had never met him. His younger brother, Harold, who was in his fifties, had been my contact with the company and was directing the rehearsal. Until the eldest Selman had elected to retire from acting a year or so earlier, he had been the star of this company. He was a most impressive man, radiating the air of a great actor. Walking with the aid of a cane, he slowly made his way to me. He seemed to be smiling, but as he approached it became clear that he was scowling. I concluded that he probably could see that I was a fake and was coming to fire me.

Mr. Selman brought his aquiline nose close to my less aquiline one, scanned my face, and instead of saying, "Get off this stage with your phony accent," said, with absolutely beautiful timbre in his voice, "Say after me!"

He delivered this as Boris Karloff might have, with an English accent and a slight lisp. "Thay after me!" is what I heard.

Frank Selman then spoke the following from what I later learned was *Richard III*. His voice boomed, spittle sprayed from his mouth—his right hand trembled as he slowly raised it. The louder he spoke, the more spittle he sprayed and the weirder he looked—one cheek going limp, one eye drooping, his contorted lips and mouth struggling to deliver these words: "Now—ith—the winter of our—dith-content," he declaimed, "May—gloriuthh—thhhummer by the thhun—of—yawwwwk . . ."

Mr. Selman stopped and said quietly, "Thay!"

I assumed two things: that Mr. Selman wanted me to "thay" what he had just said and that he wanted me to say it exactly as he had said it. I reasoned that his performance, with his face taking on a gargoyle's look, was planned—he was depicting a character who was ugly and crippled. In my mind's eye, I saw Quasimodo, replete with the hump on his back and the face Charles Laughton affected in *The Hunchback of Notre Dame*. It made great sense to me.

I, one who takes pride in being a fair impressionist, outdid myself. I channeled Mr. Selman and impersonated his voice, his grimaces, and his pantomime to perfection, palsied hand and all. My lisping on the words "discontent," "glorious," "summer," and "son of York," even to the volume of spit, was identical to his. When I finished declaiming "may gloriuthh thhhummer by the thhhhun of yawwwwwk," an eerie silence descended in the room. The dozen or so actors who had witnessed my "audition" were all staring at me. Mr. Selman too was staring at me with his good eye, the eyebrow above it fully arched.

After trying to determine whether I was a complete idiot or just an actor who follows directions too well, Mr. Selman smiled crookedly and said, "Very good, young man, very good indeed."

The most astonishing aspect of this incident was that I was blithely unaware of what I had done until a fellow actor, Gene Lyons, who would become a close and dear friend, came up to me and asked, "Hey, what the hell were you doing?"

"I was doing what he told me to do—why?"

"Mr. Selman told you to make fun of his stroke?"

I could not make Gene or anyone believe that I was not aware that our boss had suffered a major stroke. How could I notice anything about the old man when I was so busy worrying about what he was noticing about me?

What I Learned

Sometimes ignorance is bliss.

LIZ SMITH

Syndicated Columnist

W hen I began writing my nationally syndicated column back in 1976 I was almost immediately attacked publicly by a well-known publicist. For reasons best understood by him, he set out to try to destroy me, my credibility, my ethics, and, yes—even my private life.

He sent out wedding invitations that said I had married a woman, a friend, in her mother's home. He sent letters over his own signature to the head of NBC News, saying I had had someone killed. None of this was true, of course, but he never stopped!

He's still around, so far as I know. He was wrong about me being "finished" in the business, but I wasn't smart enough not to let him bother me. I once contemplated getting into his apartment secretly and painting it all in black enamel.

I fulminated against him. I tried to defend myself. I tried to punish him—to no avail. I worried and fretted. So this was a big mistake.

WHAT I LEARNED

I should have simply ignored him; let him do his worst and gone on my merry way. It is probably best to ignore your critics. Maybe they will prevail; maybe you'll be lucky, as I was, and you will prevail, but there is very little you can do to affect a matter while it is ongoing. I know Tom Cruise has been successful in suing people who offend him, and winning. But few of us have Tom's money, power, or stamina. My theory now is that you might as well be tranquil and save yourself the trouble. Let the *attack* become a part of your own fame and "legend."

Don't sue people. Don't pursue their errors. Don't defend yourself in such situations. Don't invoke the postal authorities and FBI trying to prosecute them. Don't seek revenge. Forget about it. Go on doing your thing. Become a philosopher. Realize it would never have happened in the first place if you weren't already a success.

ARTHUR HILLER

Motion Picture Director

M y mother was thirty-nine when I was born (and that was in the 1920s). I had two sisters, one thirteen years older than I and one eleven years older than I, but my parents desperately wanted to have a boy and just kept at it until I finally arrived.

I was brought up in such a protected way in such a loving home that I thought that love was just a part of family life—that everybody lived that way. Love was *just there* in our home. I remember how shocked I was when I was nine or ten and heard a classmate refer to his father as "a damn SOB." I thought, *How can someone say that about a father?* Then I met some of those damn SOB fathers and mothers and realized that not all parents were like mine.

I have such gratitude that they exposed me to so much culture. Whatever love I have for literature, for the visual arts, for music, was because of their example. They even started a Yiddish Theater in Edmonton, Alberta. They weren't professionals but they put on a play once a year just so the Jewish community could keep in touch with its cultural heritage. When I was seven or eight they let me help with painting the sets, and by the time I was ten, I was acting with the long beard and the hanging sideburns. Also, my father bought me a camera when I was six . . . a Kodak Duo 620. I loved it! By the time I was eight I had created my own darkroom in our basement so I could develop, and enlarge, my "offbeat" pictures.

More important, through their actions and comments, and without my even realizing it, my parents were instilling me with moral values. From them I learned that each person is an individual and should not be judged by color, ethnicity, or heritage. *Judge people by their actions*.

My parents had very little money but they were caring and giving . . . sometimes too much. The worst thing I ever heard my mother say about anybody was when she pointed at a newspaper picture of Adolf Hitler, in the early 1930s, and said, "He's not a nice man." I remember that my father let Joe Cotton, a ninety-year-old black man in a wheelchair, sit just inside the door of his menswear and secondhand musical instruments store for a few hours any day. Joe would just look out at the goings-on on the street or talk with my father.

Years later, when I was studying at the University of Toronto, I would travel back and forth by train. In those days the porters were all black, and the ones who were from Edmonton treated me like a king. Why? Because they all loved my father. They told me that unlike other shopkeepers, he treated them like normal folks when they went to his store. He didn't look down on them.

As I said, my parents had such wonderful moral values and tried so hard to instill them in me. I wish I could have lived up to all of them.

And what did they want me to be when I grew up? They would have supported me in whatever profession I chose, but their big desire was to see my name on the cover of a book. They meant that in a general creative sense, and were so happy to see my directing credit on TV and film.

When I began to prepare my remarks for accepting the Jean Hersholt Humanitarian Award from the Academy of Motion Picture Arts and Sciences, my love and gratitude for them came flooding back. I would be able to verbalize these regretfully unexpressed feelings to a billion people. I did . . . and somehow I feel in my heart that my parents were listening. I only wish I had said it all while they were living.

What I Learned

Express your deepest feelings to those you love while it's still possible.

DR. JOY BROWNE

Radio Psychologist

The mistake I made was getting involved with somebody who was separated when I was separated. He had been separated for nearly two years, living in a different state from his wife, when I met him. I had been living apart from my husband for a year. We got involved with each other because both of us viewed ourselves as single. The reality was that neither of us was. Separated is still married. I got divorced within the next six months, but he didn't for years. I was a public figure dating a married man. I made all the newspapers, and I am lucky the scandal didn't end my career.

What I Learned

As anyone who has ever listened to my program knows, I have the dreaded One Year Rule, which everybody hates: you have to wait a full year after a divorce or a death to start dating somebody again. Separated, staying together for the sake of the children, not having shared the same bedroom for years, afraid to leave, trying to save money, is *still married*, and as long as someone is *still married*, that person is not eligible or available as date bait. It takes a minimum of a year after the divorce is final for someone to go through an anniversary or a birthday alone, to get a cold alone, and to just be okay alone. I'm not suggesting house arrest—it's okay to hang out in groups, do volunteer activities, jog, learn Italian, work on your abs, spend some time with your mom—but your heart is going to go its own way. If the two of you had kids, they're going to have an even harder time adjusting, and they just don't get a parent dating. They'll either get too attached to or be too hostile to the new person. So do yourself and everybody a favor and wait the year after the divorce is final. View it as a road to future happiness. I wouldn't go out to lunch with somebody until I saw his final divorce decree and made sure that it was at least a year old.

BILL DANA

Comedian (José Jiménez), Writer

It was in the early seventies, and I was living in Hana, Maui—Hana, eternal entry in the Most Beautiful Place on God's Earth Contest. I had wanted to escape from all my self-inflicted sturm and tsuris (for you gentiles out there, those words mean "grief "). That's a Hana specialty, but enough time had passed. Many wounds had healed. It seemed as though my bout with Pagliacci syndrome (my name for comedian's depression) was over. I was ready to get back to work, but back to work as what? One doesn't get back to being a star of your own show. Writer! That's it! People in the industry had forgotten Bill Dana, comedy writer. And, blushes aside, not just a comedy writer but veteran writer from the original Steve Allen *Tonight Show*. Add the writer who had designed the character that became Maxwell Smart for Don Adams. The writer who had created José Jiménez. As my father would say, "Not a phony falsification."

I was the real thing. I knew that, but how could I prove it to real-thing hirers? I had been away a long time. Could I write myself back into the business? The answer was God given. The biggest television phenomenon in the country was *All in the Family*. Who's the producer? Norman Lear. What is Norman Lear to me? My oldest friend in the business, that's what. The guy who'd kept my tiny start-up career alive by hiring me as a general factotum on *The Martha Raye Show* way back in 1954.

I call, and Norman tells me up front that there's no possibility of an assignment. They have a great staff, and all the outside gigs have been assigned. "But come on in, Billy. Been too long. Love to see you."

A blur, and I'm in Mr. Lear's CBS office at Fairfax and Beverly in Los Angeles. "No chance for an episode, Bill, but it's really good to see a pal from what were Nice Old Days." Damn. Feeling low, I realize Norman doesn't know I've schlepped three thousand miles on my quest to be a scribe again.

I stand to leave. "Wait a minute. There may be something." I stop with gratitude for the delay in departure. "Got an idea. Our biggest fan is Sammy Davis. He starts his show at the Sands a half an hour late so he can tell his audience what Archie and the Bunkers are up to. There'll never be any other star on the show, but we have decided that if we can get the real Sammy Davis in the mythical Bunker household, he'll be it." Together we stumble onto the fact that Archie moonlights as a cabdriver. Everybody knows that a cabbie in Manhattan could be hailed by any star of any magnitude should geography and karma coincide. "Okay, Billy. Write a draft." I'm on my way!

Title page: "Sammy Davis Visits Archie Bunker by Bill Dana." I send in the finished script. I don't have to wait long.

"This is the best first draft we've ever had." Norman Lear is telling his Nice Old Days pal little Bill Szathmary. Not bad.

It gets better. The episode is in rehearsal. I get a call. It's Sammy! The world's greatest entertainer, his very own brilliant, loving self on the phone: "Billy boy, practice your speech. If you don't get an Emmy for this . . . well, like I say, practice your speech. We're having an absolute ball. Everybody loves it."

In order to be eligible for an Emmy a simple but critically important item called a craft card must be submitted to the appropriate guild by a specific date. I call my manager's office. He is out of town. But the devil made sure that his secretary wasn't.

Even as I type this a tingle of remembered remorse flows up the two fingers that have connected me with my muse for more than sixty years. Of course, it may be arthritis. I ask his secretary if she knows how to handle the submission transaction. "Absolutely. Piece of cake, and I hear you're a shoo-in. Consider it handled."

The show aired on February 19, 1972.

Boffo. Smasheroo. Salvos from the tube viewers.

Denouncement. The nominations for outstanding writing for a comedy series are . . . It wasn't me.

You see, my former, newest, closest secretary friend had made an error that put a stop to the glory. What had happened was, instead of the Academy of Television Arts and Sciences, home of the Emmy, she'd called Writers Guild of America, West, where a voice told her correctly that it was too early for award submissions. Not until the Emmy qualification date was already irrevocably closed and the announcements were made did we find out the source of the glitch.

There was so much excitement around that script from so many people, so much anticipation, that not being nominated had an illogical, almost incomprehensible effect on me. I returned to Hana in an emotional state I thought I had escaped.

I am a very happy man today. I am deeply in love with my wife, Evy. When you are a happy guy like me you look back and bless every cobblestone on the path that got you here. Yes, bless even those with some dreck on them. But there is a lesson from my mistake.

What I Learned

Don't buck the bromides. If it's really important to you and you want it done right, *do it yourself*.

BOBBI BROWN

Founder and CEO, Bobbi Brown Cosmetics

From the beginning of my career as a young freelance makeup artist, I was always interested in using makeup to play up a woman's natural beauty. When I did makeup, less was more: a little concealer to cover darkness under the eyes; some foundation to even out the skin; blush to create a healthy glow; and a natural lippy shade of lipstick. While many of my fellow makeup artists were contouring and painting in features, I used makeup to play up what was real.

My approach resonated with women, but one of my frustrations during those freelancing days was that I often had to "fix" most of the makeup I bought, blending it with other shades to change the tone. Store-bought foundation looked pink and chalky on the skin. Lipsticks often smelled bad or perfume-y and were either too dry or too greasy. Makeup just didn't look natural.

One day I had the idea to create a lipstick that was dense and creamy and looked like lips (only better). I made the color with the help of a chemist and I named the lipstick Brown #4. It was simple and special and looked good on many different people. Next, I thought about different women I knew and what colors would look good on them. From that came nine more shades. I now had a collection of ten lipsticks that included all tones and could be mixed and blended to create any color-correct lip shade, and in 1991, I launched Bobbi Brown Cosmetics, filling a gap in the market. The business took off and it wasn't long before other makeup companies offered their take on the "natural makeup look."

Then, in the late nineties, the pendulum swung the other way. Women wanted a cool downtown look and they started turning to younger, indie makeup companies with an edgier sensibility. I was advised that if I wanted to stay on the radar, I needed to do a dramatic about-face. Literally. I was told that women were no longer interested in neutrals and that bold was the way to go. And I listened, even though I had a nagging doubt in my gut.

In 2000, I launched an ultrabright collection of products for lips, cheeks, and eyes with shades like lemon-lime, cornflower blue, and deep magenta. The collection was a radical departure from the philosophy—a natural and simple approach to makeup—on which I'd built my company. Our ads portrayed models decked out in bright blue eye shadow, cherry bomb red lipstick, and zebra-print tops. The reaction from customers was lukewarm. Instead of looking natural, fresh, and glowing, customers were leaving our counters looking like bad makeovers.

After two seasons of lackluster sales, I knew I had made a mistake, and I quietly discontinued the new line.

What I Learned

I took a long and hard look at the decisions I'd made in the year before to figure out how we had gotten derailed. The answer was simple: I hadn't listened to my gut and I hadn't stayed true to my personal philosophy. To get back on track I needed to go back to my roots—the brand's core products. I made one simple promise that I've kept ever since: to offer only products that are 100 percent a reflection of my vision. We all have to grow and evolve—after all, that's life. The trick is to do it in a way that stays true to who you are and what's important to you.

DAN RAVIV

National Correspondent, CBS News

Live for today. Life's too short. Seize the day.

Is it really possible to encapsulate—in three words or less—the great lessons of our limited time on this planet? I've been too busy to wonder much about that, until recently.

There's nothing like a writing assignment to make you stop and smell the roses. Oops, another cliché. And yes, clichés are usually true.

Here goes: Alzheimer's. This disease really does destroy the memory part of your brain, cell by cell, lobe by lobe. Over the past two years, our family has been experiencing the effects of this illness as my father silently bids us a long good-bye.

Benjamin Raviv was born in Poland in 1925. His parents some-how knew that Europe was about to be no place for Jews. Shraga and Hannah took their little boy to British Palestine, and later they helped to make it into the State of Israel.

My mother, Esther, meantime, was taken by her parents, Eli and Raya, to Tel Aviv from Romania. They were city dwellers but also urban pioneers building a new country.

Right alongside my feeling of pride sits a huge measure of gratitude that my four grandparents made the leap of faith and left their home-towns, thus avoiding the Nazi Holocaust. Then, in 1950, my parents came to the United States—at first, only to study for a few years. I've been heard to quip that they must still be studying. Aren't we all?

My father, however, doesn't seem to be learning anymore. He was always curious and full of advice. I knew something was wrong when he stopped asking me how I got there that day, how was traffic, what's new at CBS, and a hundred other expressions of concern that could have seemed annoyingly noodgy at the time.

My mother, in the middle of all this, went through a bout of cancer—getting great and accurate chemo treatment to achieve victory. She was tenacious, she was brave, and somehow she adjusted magnificently to waging a battle without Ben actively fighting at her side. My sole brother (we enjoy that pun), Odey, gets the lion's share of credit for devotedly accompanying our mom every step of the way.

My regret is living so far away and not spending enough time with my parents. Dori and I try to explain to our kids, Jonathan and Emma, how sorry we are not to have had enough time with our loved ones who made those fateful decisions years ago that gave us freedom, safety, and comfort here in America.

As a broadcaster who is usually given precisely thirty seconds to tell a tale, I still feel childishly frustrated that there is absolutely no way to slow the hands of the clock. As the ancient Romans noted, *tempus fugit*. The best we can do is try to run and keep up.

What I Learned

Rather than being sorry we did not have enough time, we've learned to create time.

We carve out the minutes for an attentive phone call—with real listening and communication.

We find the hours for a great visit, and for us now the only way to enjoy Dad in his silence is to see him and watch his face light up when we arrive!

Devote the days to family, before the days run out. Tell all your loved ones that they are your loved ones. Brighten their lives, and thus improve your own.

ED BEGLEY JR.

Actor

When Chuck contacted me about contributing to this book, I knew that I had nothing to contribute.

I've lived a life without regrets.

And I say that with absolute certainty. One hundred percent. Not a picomicron of doubt in my mind.

And then I remembered the seventies.

I suppose I shouldn't call it regret. Let's instead call it the Zabriske Point of my own personal learning curve.

You can certainly argue that everything in your life is essential to making you the person you are today.

So, at the risk of sounding pompous (and noting that there is still much room for improvement), I *do* like who I am at this juncture.

But did I have to be such a self-absorbed dick for a whole fucking decade?

And a highly reckless one, at that. Emphasis on *high*.

Let me be clear: It's not like I broke into anyone's house or robbed a bank to support my habit. But the fact that I didn't kill anyone even when I was operating a motor vehicle on a quart of vodka a day is nothing short of miraculous.

And, while we're on the subject: Couldn't I have learned the same lessons from my father's addiction? Or from one of those educational films they showed in high school, or from David Crosby or someone?

WHAT I LEARNED

There's nothing like getting arrested or winding up in the emergency room at Cedars to make you think you might not be a "social" drinker.

BURT METCALFE

Producer and Director, Television Series *M*A*S*H*

I was a seventeen-year-old freshman in the theater arts department at UCLA, with a burning desire to be an actor. Every other freshman actor was envious of my being cast in a major stage production. It was *The Philadelphia Story*, a romantic comedy that had been the Broadway and Hollywood vehicle for Katharine Hepburn's rise to stardom.

I was to play the role of Mac, the night watchman on a big estate. I only had two lines and was onstage for just an instant, but hey: a freshman in a *major* production—now, that was big.

At the final rehearsal, the director (a faculty professor) devised and briefly rehearsed a curtain call—the actors reappearing from offstage to receive the audience's applause after the performance ends.

The cast was to file in from two doorways, one on each side of the set. As this was an arena stage with no curtain, the procedure had to be carried out in the dark. Being the actor with the smallest role, I'm the last one back from my side of the wings. I was to hold on to the hand of the actor preceding me—remember, it's pitch-dark—and with my other hand close the door behind me. The director had said this was most important, as he felt the set wouldn't look good with a door left wide open.

Opening night, the smooth performance ends with applause. Lights go black, and the cast members begin to feel their way back for the curtain call.

I hold on to the hand of the actor ahead, still knowing I have to close the door behind me. Now, here's where I make a fatal mistake. In reaching for the doorknob, I somehow lose the guiding hand in front, but I close that damn door. Still in the dark, I edge my way further onstage to catch up with the group. Unknowingly, I've gone just in front of the person I was to be alongside of, and kept moving laterally. As the lights come up, Burt Metcalfe, with his two-line part, is standing all alone, dead center stage, while the entire remaining cast is lined up behind him!

If only the floor could open up and swallow me whole. Talk about wanting to be dead last.

WHAT I LEARNED

Maybe I wasn't meant to be an actor. Although I did act professionally for several years thereafter in theater, film, and TV, I finally decided to give up that dream and pursue a career on the production side of show business. That seemed to work out better.

ERNIE ALLEN

President and CEO, National Center for Missing and Exploited Children

I am a native of Louisville, Kentucky. I grew up just three blocks north of historic Churchill Downs, the mecca of thoroughbred racehorses, home of the Kentucky Derby. Many of my early jobs were at Churchill Downs, and to this day it holds a special place in my heart.

My favorite time at Churchill Downs was not in the afternoon, when the races were run and the grandstands filled. I liked the early mornings. The back side of a racetrack is like a small self-contained city, a melting pot of people and animals. There, each morning, in close proximity, one could find the low-wage stable hands, the exercise riders, the superstar jockeys, the fiercely competitive trainers, the wealthy owners, the veterinarians, and many others.

Every morning, 365 days a year, it happens. Trainers prepare their horses. Exercise riders and jockeys gallop the horses or give them brisk workouts to build speed and endurance. The stable hands cool the horses after their exertion, bathe them, groom them, and prepare them for the future. It is a unique scene, unmatched anywhere else.

I was always concerned about the welfare of the stable workers. Most of them were virtual migrant workers, moving from track to track as one race meeting ended and another began, living in cramped quarters on or near the racetrack. Most of them lacked the basic necessities of life. They were of all ages and races, and I was particularly concerned about the older workers, most of whom could not look forward to pensions or an easy retirement.

One morning more than thirty years ago, I entered the track kitchen, a place where everyone from the humblest stable hand to the most powerful owner came together for breakfast. There were no reserved tables. When someone got up to leave, you sat down regardless of who else might be at the table.

On this morning I noticed an empty chair next to an elderly, unshaven, somewhat disheveled-looking man. He was wearing a floppy brimmed hat and a heavy coat and was alone. I asked if I might join him. He agreed quietly and I sat down to eat my breakfast.

We cautiously began a conversation and spoke about a wide range of things. We never introduced ourselves. I was concerned that he might have no money and not be able to afford something to eat. At the track kitchen, there were no free refills. So as I rose to go back to the counter and buy a second cup of coffee, I asked, "May I get you something?" He answered, "A cup of coffee would be nice."

So I bought him a cup of coffee. We conversed some more, and again I asked if I could get him something else. Again he accepted a refill of his coffee.

Finally, I rose to leave, wished him well, and headed for the exit. At the door I was joined by a local trainer whom I knew well. He asked me, "How do you know Mr. Galbreath?" I answered, "Who?" He responded, "The man you were sitting with is John W. Galbreath, the chairman of the board of Churchill Downs."

I was stunned. Mr. Galbreath was not only chairman of Churchill Downs, he was a multimillionaire, a builder of skyscrapers around the world, a friend of presidents and royalty, owner of the Pittsburgh Pirates for forty years, owner of Darby Dan Farm, and breeder and owner of two Kentucky Derby winners and one Epsom Derby winner.

I was buying coffee, offering a free breakfast, and feeling pity for one of the world's richest and most powerful men. It was very early in the morning. He had not yet shaved or prepared for his day. He was not dressed as I would have expected one of the most powerful, influential people in the world to be dressed.

What I Learned

My chance encounter with John W. Galbreath taught me a lesson I have never forgotten. One cannot make assumptions about people based on how they look. I now strive to treat every person with dignity and respect, no matter who I think they are, and to respond to each encounter with another human being with kindness and an open mind.

As for Mr. Galbreath, who passed away in 1988 at the age of ninety, I will never forget him or our brief time together. One writer called him "the nicest, most unpretentious, most hospitable man you'll ever encounter." I can attest to that, and to the fact that my few minutes with him changed my life.

BILL D'ELIA

Director, Writer, Producer

A few years ago, while sitting around the dinner table, my son Christopher, then twenty years old, said that he thought a good idea for a television series would be a behind-the-scenes look at a play being produced. The idea of the nonsense and shenanigans that go on to mount a production of anything seemed to him to be full of possibilities. As we discussed it, I thought that it should be a Broadway play and that we should never actually see the play but end every episode with the curtain going up. That way we would only see the behind-the-scenes soap opera and not the actual play. It was a fun discussion, and the idea stuck with me.

I couldn't stop thinking about it, and eventually thought that if we told the story through the eyes of an understudy, it could be a fun and interesting show. And what if the show were a musical? And what if our series was musical as well?

At the time I was executive producer and director of the TV show *Ally McBeal*, a show full of fun and musical ideas. I took the understudy idea to David E. Kelley, creator of *Ally* and a guy who knows a thing or two about television and music. He immediately liked the idea and mulled over the possibility of writing it himself. He decided he'd like to produce it, but we'd need to find a writer. After interviewing many writers and reading lots of scripts, we made a deal with the writer Ivan Menchell. Together we cracked the story, figured out the musical possibilities, and went with David to pitch the series.

We sold it immediately to the Fox network and began to work on the script. This was great news, and I couldn't wait to share it with everyone. I told Chris and he wanted to know what that meant, and I told him that I thought we could somehow work on this together. My son Matt called shortly thereafter. Matt was a student at NYU then, studying film. Matt told me that he and Chris were upset with me. Why?

Well, I'd stolen Chris's idea.

His idea? All he did was say, "Hey, Dad, what about this?" at the dinner table. How was that his idea? I was furious that Matt and Chris were furious. In my defense, this is what I do for a living, and we talk about these things at home all the time. The fact that this discussion led me to form a fully fleshed-out idea seemed not to be a problem to me at all. Matt said, "What if you were at the dinner table with a friend? And what if the friend had the same idea? Would you not have included your friend in the pitch?" Chris didn't want to "somehow work on this together"—the whole idea was for us to create a show and crack the story as partners. I had excluded him right from the start and found another partner. When I stepped back and looked at it, I realized that my sons were right and I was wrong. I called Chris and apologized for what I had done. It still pains me to think about it, and it's still a very difficult thing to admit.

And by the way, the show didn't get picked up by Fox, was then sold to ABC, was rewritten several times, was hailed as "breakthrough television" by at least one network executive, and was never produced.

What I Learned

Well, I learned many things. First, that as my boys grew into men, I had to grow with them. I learned to see them as equals and friends, not just as my sons. I learned to listen to them as I would any colleague and not as if I always knew best just because I was the dad. Additionally, I learned that they were protective of, and loyal to, each other, and that made me very proud. A side benefit of all that learning: I have a movie in production that Chris wrote and I will direct, and I'm producing a movie that Matt will write and direct. I guess the other thing I learned is that maybe I should have had more kids. They have good ideas.

ROBERT TOWNE

Academy Award–Winning Screenwriter

My first exposure to Robert Evans was after I'd written what became known as the garden scene between Al Pacino and Marlon Brando in *The Godfather*. Francis Ford Coppola was about to show the film for the first time to Paramount in the form of studio head Evans and his wife, Ali McGraw. It was to take place in a little screening room on Canon Drive in Beverly Hills. Francis was suddenly rather nervous as he heard something in the hall that attracted his attention. I looked down the hall and there, being wheeled down a crimson carpet, wearing silk pajamas, was Evans.

Obviously in severe pain, he was wheeled into the room and it was literally, "Oh, my aching back! I can't move." It was then, as he was lifted out of the wheelchair into the cushy studio seats that I noticed the little slippers with the gold brocaded foxes on the toes. Before I'd really had a chance to absorb the fact that this was the guy who was going to judge the film for the studio, Evans started to suck his thumb—audibly. Worse yet, he started to hum. I looked over to Francis, and he looked like a basset hound who'd just been kicked in the nuts. In other words, he was thinking what I was thinking: *This is a fucking catastrophe and the film hasn't even started*.

Three and a half hours later the film was over. I had no idea what Evans was going to say. It was public knowledge that he and Francis had had a rough time on the film. But Evans proceeded quietly and clearly: "There's too much spaghetti eating, there's too much music," and so he went through the film, incisive and insightful. I thought, *This can't be possible,* but there it was. Drooling royalty is trundled into the room, takes its thumb out of its mouth, and responds with a kind of reflexive brilliance.

Francis was there arguing with him and I finally said, "Francis, I think he's right." I was a little embarrassed; Francis is my friend and I was there for support. I could only conclude that appearances were deceiving and that underneath the slick Brylcreamed hair and black outfits there was this idiot savant who, once you got him in front of the film, was amazing. He was completely in touch with his own feelings, and nothing stood in the way of his expressing them.

That was the beginning of a relationship with him that led me to *Chinatown.* I've subsequently made fun of our first meeting, how all through the making of *Chinatown* Evans never understood the script, never pretended to understand the script—he just liked the title and that's all there was to it. And over the years, hanging out in his projection room, I became privy to his endless fund of self-deprecating stories, many of which wound up in his book, *The Kid Stays in the Picture.* How elaborate preparations were made for one of his marriages and the prospective bride backed out of the wedding, and Evans could only kvetch and moan, "What am I going to do? The invitations have already gone out!" How his household staff worried every time he drove himself to the studio from his Beverly Hills home because he tended to get lost anywhere east of Doheny Drive.

So when it came time to do *Chinatown*'s sequel, *The Two Jakes,* we knew who Jake Gittes was going to be, but for the other Jake, Berman, the thought of Evans in the part seemed like an idea whose time had come. We all—including Evans—knew that he had been a terrible actor in his youth, but the Evans that I saw night after night regaling us with these masochistic tales was so charming that I thought it would make a great facade for a character who had, as Jake Berman had, a hidden agenda—a dying man trying to cover it up. I thought it would be wonderful if we could just get the Evans that talked about himself that way in his projection room—on film opposite Jack Nicholson. I made the suggestion.

Now, all too often the difference between a brilliant idea and a mistake is that you only know which is which after the fact. All the reasons for doing it were great. (And all the reasons for not doing it were great as well.) I broached the idea and Nicholson thought it was wonderful. So I sat down with Evans, who would be not only acting in the film but producing it as well, and I said, "I don't know if this is going to work out, but if it is we're going to need to rehearse intensely for two months. Can you do that?" No problem. He could. I asked Jack. No problem. He could as well. I also warned Evans, "If I don't think it's working, I want to be free to come and tell you. I need to have the freedom to say so." Absolutely. He agreed.

Then we got involved in preproduction, and *any* preproduction can be very trying. In this case our production was a negative pickup, so we were not going to get actual production money until we started shooting. Naturally, this made everyone nervous in that you-can't-get-there-from-here state that is the lot of all movies that must run their preproduction tank on empty until the first day of shooting. But everyone involved—the costume people, set designers, and so on—kept us going even though the picture was already running up quite a debt before we officially had our funding on the first day of production.

However, while I was seeing to all the details of preproduction, my two stars decided that they needed to go off for a bit—Jack went skiing in Aspen and Evans too said he needed a little break. I said, "Where are you going?" He said, "Tahiti." So the planned rehearsals between Jack and Bob were not exactly practical or possible under these conditions. When Evans finally returned from Tahiti some six weeks later, it was immediately evident that he was not looking to give us the charming, self-deprecating schmendrick that we had all come to know and love but the dazzling leading man that he hadn't been twenty years earlier.

That clearly was not what I was looking for, and I didn't think it would work—especially since the actual rehearsal time had shrunk from two months to two weeks. One of the things that concerned me most was the rate at which Evans spoke. Not only was it twice as fast as anyone else, but he mumbled—in fact, Dustin Hoffman had Evans very much in mind when he played the character Mumbles in *Dick Tracy*. Evans, in a word, was difficult to understand and impossible to slow down.

I was kind of beside myself, so, after having done some camera tests to see how he looked on film and trying to rehearse with him, I realized he saw the character as the preening mobster Bugsy Siegel, while I saw the character as much closer to his humorous if thuggish capo, Mickey Cohen. It really came down to the fact that I was going to have to ask the producer to replace one of the leading actors—namely, himself.

So I went over to his house and sat in his bedroom on top of his black mink fur spread (he was sitting in bed under it) and said, "Bob, look: We talked about this a long time ago; we agreed that if there was ever a difficulty the most important thing was the picture and we would agree to make a change. And we need to protect the picture and there's just no time. We have a tight schedule and there's so much work for us to do, I don't know how we can possibly do it in the time we have, and furthermore, I'm going to need a real *producer* on the film, and you're the producer, so I don't see how it's possible that you can do everything that needs to be done to play this part and produce the picture . . ." I went on and on in this fashion, citing the reasons from every department why this change had to be made. I must have talked nonstop for an hour, and he looked and listened, and after I stopped he said to me, "So what are you saying?"

Well, that was the beginning of the end. The project unraveled in a rather spectacular way and none of us spoke to each other for years.

Now, I have no idea what the movie would have been like having cast someone else as Berman at the beginning, but I finally saw an inkling of the performance I would have liked in *The Kid Stays in the Picture,* where Evans was relaxed and in high self-deprecating good humor, everything I wanted him to be as Jake Berman. I'm afraid the only person who could get Evans to be Evans was Evans himself.

WHAT I LEARNED

I don't know that there's any one lesson that can be taken away from *The Two Jakes,* partly because the mistakes are so numerous in a situation like this, it's hard to point to one in particular except for the first one: if I hadn't suggested Evans to Evans to begin with, it need never have happened. I had revived a nearly forgotten dream that Evans had of being a leading man, one he had been more than willing to forget had I not been foolish enough to say, "Of course you can do it!"

But the thing about a movie is that you have to make mistakes to get a movie made. The question isn't whether you're going to make them; you're going to make them at twenty-four frames a second. The moviemaking process by its very nature is a forgiving one. That's why you have the capacity for endless numbers of takes; that's why you have an editor standing by to remake the movie in endless ways. If thirty takes are mistakes, there's always the thirty-first—that's what the process is for.

In fact, what makes a movie work best, I think, is how quickly and effectively you can make mistakes, how quickly you can go down wrong paths that can strongly suggest the right path. They say writing is rewriting. Well, it's the same thing with a movie, only more so. Making good movies is making mistakes fast enough to correct them. If you can't correct your mistakes on a movie, then you've subverted the entire wacky Rube Goldberg process of moviemaking: you've made the biggest mistake of all—being in a position that doesn't allow for mistakes.

In many ways I owe Evans my career for his championing *Chinatown* at a time when and a place where the studio understood it even less than he did. And fortunately, the one mistake Evans and I never made was losing our friendship. We sure as hell bent it on *The Two Jakes,* but it was never broken.

KENNETH COLE

Designer

In 1986 I was asked to give a speech about my involvement with the American Foundation for AIDS Research (amfAR) at Carnegie Hall in front of more than a thousand members of the arts community. I declined. I'm not a public speaker. It's just not what I do, or, as with most people, what I'm in any way comfortable doing. I'd just become engaged in the battle against HIV/AIDS (recently running my first public service campaign about the disease) and was still educating myself. I was sure they could find someone more qualified.

But then the event organizer, Fred, came to see me. He was so animated and persuasive that I just couldn't say no. I asked him what I was supposed to say, and he told me to just tell them what I do and why. It seemed straightforward, and it seemed to be something that would not likely take a lot, if any, preparation, so I reluctantly agreed to make the speech.

Still, I was worried. Should I write a speech or not? I knew this stuff, but would I be too nervous to deliver it well? Maria Cuomo, whom I had recently started dating, suggested I start by acknowledging and thanking Fred for making the night possible. After all, he would not likely get the credit he deserved. It would also give me some time to relax before I actually got into my presentation, or speech, or whatever it was.

So that night I followed Dr. Mathilda Krim, the founder of

amfAR, and preceded Ali Gertz, a young woman who had contracted HIV very early on and had shared her story with whomever she could, becoming an icon in the process. I took the stage at Carnegie Hall in front of several thousand people, without notes. Because of the footlights I couldn't see past five feet in front of me and all I could hear was the ocean of noise, a buzz out there in that vast hall. I started as planned by praising Fred. "Thanks to Fred's effort this event had become possible," and so on. I seemed to be getting great feedback. Out there in the haze the room was buzzing, so I said even more about him—"After all, this night was really very much about Fred"—and then more, and with each reference an even more pronounced buzz from the audience. I felt I had hit a home run with my praise of Fred. This gave me the confidence I needed. Now relaxed, I delivered my message, and it seemed to go well.

I finished the speech exhilarated and relieved, and grateful to Maria for her advice. When I returned to my seat somewhere in the middle of the vast hall, Maria passed me a note. "You were great, but his name is not Fred."

My family had a field day with my error. It was clear they would never let me live this down. My renaming of Fred at Carnegie Hall was the story that was recited at family dinners and all holiday gatherings.

Fred's actual name was Peter—not even close. I wasn't sure if Peter had been terribly offended by my blunder or not, but I chose to let it go, knowing that there was not much I could do about it at that point. Peter's feelings eventually became clear. All present were urged to fill out a form attached to their programs with their addresses, so they could each receive a video of the event. When it arrived all presentations were beautifully edited, except for one, which was just omitted.

Two years passed after that night at Carnegie Hall, and my sister, Abbie, who had been present for the mishap, called to tell me she had just read in the *New York Times* that Peter Glen, that evening's inspiring host, had passed away. I was saddened that this great AIDS advocate had left us.

I used that story for the next several years when I spoke in public. It always helped relax me and ease into my subject, which was usually about the importance of AIDS awareness. I would say, ". . . and Maria passed me the note, and it read . . . 'but his name is not Fred.'" I would then pause, usually after a laugh, and say, "His name in fact was Peter Glen, and he has since died of AIDS."

I delivered this message to probably a few thousand people over about a five- to eight-year period, and after having just done it again at the opening of my new store in Los Angeles, I was back in my office in New York. In the middle of a meeting my assistant popped her head into my office and said, "Kenneth, Peter Glen is on the line for you."

I didn't take the call. I needed a bit of composure and a lot of research before I could speak to whoever was on the other end of the call.

He hadn't died after all. It turned out that it was another Peter Glen who in fact had died. It also turned out that this Peter Glen wasn't particularly happy with his twenty-some-odd premature eulogies. Although he was an inspiring man, he understandably didn't have a sense of humor that would accept my gaffe.

So the facts are, I didn't just humiliate myself in front of thousands of people, but I also buried a great man years before he actually passed.

What I Learned

Spend more time on preparation.

RICHARD MARTINI

Filmmaker

Nothing prepares you for the cacophony of India. A sea of mini-cabs, multicolored trucks, water buffaloes, camels, elephants, and an occasional vulture clog its dusty roads with endless bleating and honking. I had flown into India for a trip exploring the former Tibetan state of Ladakh with Sanjay Saxena, tour group leader and native of Delhi, and Robert Thurman, professor of Tibetan philosophy at Columbia University. They were leading us on our journey through Ladakh's ancient Tibetan monasteries and then up to Dharamsala to see the Dalai Lama.

While traipsing through a magnificent sixteenth-century monastery outside of Thikse, I bumped my head in a small stupa, or ceremonial burial site. I looked down to find two penny-size painted stones at my feet. I've traveled a bit around the planet, and have a habit of taking pocket-size pebbles as souvenirs of my journey, from the pyramids of Giza to the Great Wall of China. So when I reached down and admired these hand-painted pieces of clay, I didn't think much about pocketing them.

Later, Professor Thurman was taking us through the inner sanctuary of a Buddhist temple, and I saw a painting on the wall depicting humans being tortured, flayed, and devoured by demons. "This painting shows what happens to those who disturb these sacred grounds," he said. Suddenly my penchant for souvenir grabbing seemed to take on a dark tone; maybe having a pair of souvenir stones wasn't such a good idea.

After rafting the Indus and camping under glorious skies, we headed for Dharamsala, home of the Dalai Lama. Driving in India is a driver's education class nightmare. Animals and owners dart in front of cars at will; roads are littered with the losers of the daily battles. While driving through one of these villages, a boy suddenly darted in front of our Jeep. The driver swerved, saving the young boy's life, but the boy slammed into my door and crumpled under the car. His foot was badly wounded; with sinew and bone breaking through his ankle, the boy writhed in pain.

Sanjay quickly pulled him into the car and drove us to a nearby hospital. We escorted him to the emergency room and were lucky to find a surgeon on call who went to work immediately. Sanjay and Professor Thurman arranged payments for a year of therapy in advance, as well as compensation to his family. However, I feared the culprit was really me. Ever since I'd picked up those stones, I was waiting for an accident to happen. As I considered pitching them, my Western mind argued with me: *Unlucky stones? Stones aren't unlucky. It was an accident,* I thought. I figured we were on our way to Dharamsala, and there must be a temple where I could return them. Back into my pocket they went.

Suddenly there was a loud explosion. A huge main electrical wire that went from the hospital into town exploded overhead in a shower of sparks. The whipping wire flew down from the pole and snaked across the entrance, sending sparks and flames as it went, until it came to rest over the main gate to the hospital. There was no way for us to leave. We quickly assessed what to do, and while the group was trying to figure out what that was, I tiptoed away and reached into my pocket, determined to rid myself of the bad karma of these mystical stones.

I saw a fountain nearby and placed them on the stone edge. I looked around to make sure no one saw me, and felt I had gotten away with ridding myself of what was obviously causing misfortune. Brushing my hands clean of their blue and white dust, I breathed a sigh of relief. Even if they had no power, I was happy to not have them in my pocket. A few minutes later, we searched for a safer, nonelectrified exit. Some group members and I walked back past the fountain, looking for another way out of the hospital entrance, and I casually glanced over to where I'd set the stones down seconds before. They had vanished.

I looked around the grounds to see if anyone could've taken them, but the parking lot was empty—there was no way in and no way out. These magical stones had simply disappeared into thin air. I went over to look again. There wasn't a trace of them having been there. Had they been picked up by a crow? Had they somehow dissolved into the moisture that was on the fountain ledge? Perhaps they'd just flown back to Ladakh. I'll never know.

We finally made it to our hotel in Dharamsala, where I eagerly took a shower. As I got out and was traversing the damp concrete floor, I turned on a lamp and suddenly was aware my hand was stuck to it. I felt my arm go numb and realized I was being electrocuted. After a few seconds of panic, I swung my free arm around and smashed it against the hand that was unable to let go of the lamp. The resulting flash knocked me off my feet and onto the floor. Celestial payback for having disturbed a shrine? I don't know, but I had literally gotten the shock of my life, albeit a shock of enlightenment.

What I Learned

What I learned—as I lay there on the floor—was that it's better to leave things undisturbed, in their natural state, than to claim them as souvenirs. As it is with our planet—and its environment—maybe it's better to leave things as we find them so that others may come and enjoy them after we're gone. Whether it's an Alaskan wilderness or two tiny Tibetan stones. As it turns out, this story's become a better souvenir of my trip to India than any rock, but it also serves as a lamppost for an old Indian maxim: "Never stand on concrete in wet bare feet when turning on a lamp."

WALLY SCHIRRA

One of the Original Seven Astronauts, Mercury, Gemini, and Apollo Missions

I was a naval aviator test pilot at Patuxent River Naval Air Test Center when I was ordered to report to Washington, D.C., with a group of military test pilots. Two engineers and a psychiatrist lectured us about going into space on top of a rocket in a capsule. I immediately thought of the clown who is shot out of a cannon at the circus and thought, *No way*. Then they continued with the remark that they would send monkeys and chimpanzees first. I wanted out of there. After we returned to the test center, my colleagues pointed out that if I wanted to go higher, farther, and faster, this was the way. I accepted the invitation.

WHAT I LEARNED

First feelings are often misleading.

SCOTT CARPENTER

One of the Original Seven Astronauts, Mercury Mission

I went to Los Angeles in the 1960s and I was staying with my friend the comedian and comedy astronaut Bill Dana (José Jiménez). We would stroll down the Sunset Strip and look at the girls and enjoy their looks back. Two decades later I returned to Los Angeles to start a business in oceanography. Again I stayed with my friend Bill, and again we strolled down the Sunset Strip and looked at the girls, but this time they didn't look back.

WHAT I LEARNED

I was born too long ago.

ANDREW H. TISCH

Chairman, Executive Committee for Loews Corporation

Until March 12, 1991, I was invincible, or so I thought. I was going through a "let's go get scared" phase of my life and was willing to try anything.

That is, until I tried helicopter skiing. I went to the Bugaboos in the Canadian Rockies on a one-week trip with Canadian Mountain Holidays, the largest helicopter skiing outfit, and one of the most reputable. I was there to try something new, to push the envelope, and to experience wide-open skiing. All over the brochures were the warnings about how dangerous the sport is and the possible consequences. I ignored every one of them. I ignored the pleas of my family and my then girlfriend (now wife). I ignored my own instincts. I went with some trepidation. But I went—in part because I did not want to disappoint the rest of our group of friends, who were counting on me.

We got there on a Saturday—flying to Calgary, busing five hours to a siding on a back road, and flying twenty-five minutes by helicopter to the lodge. We learned about deep-snow rescue. On Sunday we skied at lower altitudes because it was snowing heavily. We skied among the trees, and I was having some difficulty mastering the concept of deep-powder skiing because the snow was so heavy. I struggled on Sunday and again on Monday, never feeling quite comfortable about how I was skiing or about the way the group was being asked to ski by the expert guide leading us.

On Tuesday, the heavy snow stopped and we got what we came for—high-altitude skiing on glaciers in champagne powder. The kind that stings your lungs when you inhale. The kind you can dance through. The kind you see in a Warren Miller film. And the skiing was great. But there was something about the leadership of the group of eleven skiers that did not sit right with me. The guide kept on saying, "I'll see you at the bottom" and skiing away, expecting everyone to find him farther down the mountain at the helicopter meeting point in some unknown place. But the thrill of skiing the deep powder was powerful.

By lunchtime, my legs were really hurting from the exertion and the thrills. As we skied down to the middle of a field for lunch, I saw my lodge roommate and great friend, David Karetsky, sitting on a chair made from his skis and canvas. Giving him my best macho voice, I said, "Does it get any better than this?" He answered, "This is as good as it gets." I moved on and ate lunch with some of the others. After lunch, I conceded to myself that I shouldn't ski any longer as my legs were really hurting. The helicopter was going back to the lodge to refuel, and some of the others were feeling the same exhaustion I felt, so I went in to a take a nap.

As I lay in bed, I was unable to fall asleep. My mind was racing from the exhilaration of the morning. Then my mind shifted to the discomfort I was feeling and the idea that there were so many ways in which I could get hurt helicopter skiing—crash, unmarked object, tree well, cliff, rock, you name it. Finally, I thought about everyone back in New York who'd told me not to go and if I did go to be careful not to ski outside my comfort level. I decided I would leave the lodge immediately and head back to New York, three days early. There was a helicopter going to the road, where I would call a taxi to take me the five hours to Calgary.

As I was putting my bag onto the helicopter, the entire staff came running out, threw my bag off the chopper, and told me there had been an accident and they needed the chopper to get to the scene. About an hour later I found out that nine of my fellow skiers had been killed in an avalanche—including my good friend who'd said, "This is as good as it gets."

I never saw the accident scene. I only saw one of the "Skadi" transponders, which are used to locate avalanche victims. They are made of unbreakable plastic, but this one was mangled.

As I traveled back to New York from Calgary in a mournful daze, I went through my trip file. I came across a *Sports Illustrated* article written about five months earlier, about a Canadian Mountain Holiday trip in the Bugaboos on which someone had died. On the article was a Post-it note from me to David Karetsky reading, "David, this looks pretty dangerous. Do you really think we should do it? See you in Calgary."

WHAT I LEARNED

Trust your instincts. Something told me that this was not a good idea. All my defenses were talking to me and telling me to stop—my legs, my racing mind, my inability to sleep, my family and those who loved me. Finally, I woke up to the signals and let my instincts take over.

RICHARD ZOGLIN

Time Magazine Critic

Critics don't like to admit mistakes. Indeed, it's part of the critic's very DNA to try to maintain the illusion that you're incapable of them. A critic's job is to convince readers, in the most colorful and convincing language possible, that his or her opinion is the only one any sensible person could hold. And nothing that happens afterward can prove you wrong. So what if the gritty police drama you hailed is canceled after two weeks, or the sitcom you trashed becomes a runaway hit? It's the audience that fouled up, not you.

For a dozen years I was the television critic for *Time* magazine. I privately cheered when shows I praised from the start—*Thirtysomething, ER*—went on to have long and acclaimed runs. I was just as happy when I was a lonely voice of dissent. I still think *Amerika*—the 1987 ABC miniseries about a Soviet takeover of the United States that bombed in the ratings despite my raves—was an underrated gem. And my snarky review of *Friends* in 1995? I still wish I could have strangled that show in its cradle. But one review remains a thorn in my side, mainly because I dumped on a show that later became one of my favorites, the only network series that today, nearly a decade after I left the TV beat, I still make sure to watch or tape every week: *The Simpsons.*

I watched Matt Groening's animated segments on the old *Tracey Ullman Show,* which introduced the Simpsons characters, and I was unimpressed: lots of belching and shouting, juvenile jokes, and crass drawings. When the half-hour series debuted on Fox in January 1990 and became a pop culture phenomenon—high ratings, T-shirts, catchphrases like "eat my shorts"—I was even more turned off.

I resisted even reviewing the show initially, then included it in an April 1990 story on "anti-family sitcoms," lumping it in with *Roseanne* and *Married with Children*. I had a few nice things to say about the show, but I made my dissenting view clear: "*The Simpsons*, however, is strangely off-putting much of the time. The drawings are grotesque without redeeming style or charm and the animation is crude even by TV's low-grade standards." I refused to put *The Simpsons* on my 10 Best list at the end of the year. Instead, I found Bart Simpson a place on another list—as the "Most Overexposed Underachiever" of the year. (Bart still wound up on *Time*'s cover that week. Ah, the follies of newsmagazine cover making. But that's another essay.)

I started to come around a year or two later. I still insist the show got better, as the emphasis shifted from Bart, the wisecracking brat, to Homer, the doughnut-loving dunderhead. The characters deepened; the satire grew denser and more audacious. And yes, even the animation got better. Still, it would have been nice if I had recognized *The Simpsons'* spark of originality the first time around, before the rest of the world did. If there's anything a critic likes less than being wrong, it's looking like a bandwagon-hopper.

What I Learned

A critic's opinion can change. We can even make mistakes. Which is why readers shouldn't take us too seriously.

PHIL MUSHNICK

New York Post Sports Columnist

My biggest mistake came the day I, now a sportswriter with more than thirty years on the job, said yes to Jimmy "the Greek" Snyder, at the time the noted tout on CBS's *NFL Today*.

It was a mistake I learned from. Heck, I didn't duplicate it until, oh, an entire day later, when I again said yes to Jimmy the Greek.

In 1983, as a kid sports columnist for the *New York Post*, I wrote a piece that, for better or worse, endeared me to Snyder. It was about how, for all his fame and fleeting fortune, nobody knew the troubles he'd seen: Two of his children had died from cystic fibrosis. A third, hospitalized with the disease, was slipping.

The Greek was touched, so much so that I couldn't lose him. He'd call three, four times a week, inviting me to join him at the racetrack, a casino, in Miami or Vegas, bill it all to him.

He thought that everyone shared his reality, that anyone could just pick up and leave. And he did not, for a second, even try to understand that as a journalist I could not accept such favors from those I covered.

One night in 1985, the Greek called from Louisville, where he'd be working the Kentucky Derby telecast that weekend for CBS. He insisted that I immediately fly down as his guest. No way, I told him. I again had to explain it to him. Besides, I told him, there was a press conference I had to cover the next day, in Manhattan, at the Americana Inn.

"You're kidding," Snyder replied. "I've got a friend staying there. He's a prince, a real prince, from some kingdom somewhere. He's got a package for me. I'll arrange for you to pick it up. Okay?"

"Sure, no problem."

The Greek's princely pal—I never got the name, just the room number—was staying in a penthouse suite, closer to outer space than to the lobby. I rode the elevator, walked a hallway, went around a corner, knocked on the door.

The door was opened by a huge man, built like an anvil, but he wasn't as big as the other guy in the room. Both glared at me as if they couldn't help it. I figured them for bodyguards. Or murderers. Or both.

A nearly naked young woman was seated in one corner of the room. I figured her for the princess. Or a hooker.

The "prince," a light-skinned black man (or dark-skinned white man), was summoned from a side room. In a French accent, he asked me for identification. Huh?

"What do you need my ID for? I was sent here by the Greek; you were expecting me, no?"

"How do I know you are who you say?"

"I never said I am who I am."

Seeing how I never play a small room well anyway, I produced ID. The prince nodded at one of his XXXL boys, and he began to display the contents of "the package." On the couch, next to the princess, they counted out stacks of hundred-dollar bills, ten to a stack, twenty stacks. Good grief—$20,000 in cash, more money, by about $19,900, than I'd ever even had in my pocket. By "package," I'd thought, I don't know, maybe a nice shirt.

"Now you count it," the prince ordered. I complied, all the time thinking, *What the hell is going on and why is it going on with me?*

The prince put the money in a brown paper shopping bag, had me sign a receipt, and then handed me the bag. Time to go. Whew.

But as I was leaving, it hit me: I'd just signed for the money and now these guys were going to follow me, then roll me for it. No, kill

me for it. I walked out of the penthouse, then pivoted in the opposite direction of the elevator, figuring that they figured I'd be headed
back the same way from which I came.

I entered an emergency exit staircase, ran down several flights of
steps, then reentered the hotel's hallway and ran in no particular
direction before entering another emergency staircase and running
down a few more flights. I must've repeated this process ten times
before—sweaty, breathless, and too young to die—I walked through
an emergency door and into a ground-floor kitchen in the Americana Inn.

Forget the press conference; I wanted out, and immediately. I
headed home to New Jersey, confident that I'd cheated death but not
at all pleased to be carrying $20,000 in hundred-dollar bills (for an
on-person total of $20,009).

When I got home, I called the Greek in Louisville. "Listen, you
didn't tell me what was in the prince's package. It makes me nervous.
First thing in the morning, I'm going to deposit it, then send you a
check."

"No!" the Greek hollered. "You can't do that!"

The Greek went on to explain that he liked a bunch of Kentucky-
breds on the next day's Derby Day card and that they'd pay more at
a New York off-track betting parlor than at Churchill Downs, and
how he didn't want to bet a lot down there, not with all the CBS
execs around him. He pleaded with me.

"You live just across the bridge from an OTB, don'tcha?"

And then I did it again: I said yes to the Greek.

Snyder began to read off all kinds of combination bets for six or
seven races—$2,500 exactas, $1,000 trifecta boxes, a $2,000 "reverse
wheel"—and I dutifully wrote them all down. Thankfully, he
stopped dictating his action when he reached twenty grand.

The next day, cursing myself along the way, I drove to an OTB
parlor on Staten Island. I got in line at the window, two pages of bets
and my brown paper shopping bag—now double-lined—in hand.

When I reached the teller, I began: "The first race today at Churchill
Downs, exacta box B, C, and F, two thousand dollars . . ."

The teller went from looking down and uninterested to looking up and agitated. "Whoa, pal, you can't just make that kind of bet at this window!"

"Why not?"

"'Cause I'm not going to punch a ticket for that kinda money until I see you have the money to cover it."

I beckoned him closer, then let him peek into my shopping bag. He looked up at me, and then, his eyes still on me, hollered, "Gloria!"

Gloria, about sixty and a woman who had the look of a veteran of racetrack welfare, stepped forward from a back room. The teller whispered to her. She nodded, then looked at me.

"Come down here with me," she said.

We went to a betting window at the far right side of the OTB, a window she opened just for me. I restated the recitation of the Greek's bets. We counted out the money together after every bet, and then she punched out the tickets and gave them to me.

About halfway through the Greek's twenty grand, Gloria looked up. "Sonny," she said, "this isn't your money, is it?"

I'd been waiting for that, hoping for that. Knowing she wouldn't believe me, I told her the truth.

"Nah, it's Jimmy the Greek's."

"Yeah, right," she grunted, as if she figured she deserved a silly, wise-guy answer to her silly question. Then we went back to work.

The Greek, it turned out, didn't cash a single bet. All losers, $20,000 worth of losing tickets. I still have a stack of them, as souvenirs of the time I twice, on consecutive days, said yes to Jimmy the Greek.

When I next spoke to the Greek I told him that I'd someday like to write about our little two-day episode.

"Wait till I die," he growled.

"It's a deal," I said.

On April 21, 1996, eleven years later and at the age of seventy-six, Dimetrios Georgios Synodinos—Jimmy "the Greek" Snyder—died. That day, I wrote the story for the next day's newspaper.

WHAT I LEARNED

And so what did I learn from this experience? What can we all learn from it? For starters, try to avoid situations in which you think there's a good chance you'll be murdered. Second, it's amazing how many hundred-dollar bills can fit into a brown paper shopping bag. Try it yourself. Third . . .

VICKI L. MABREY

Nightline Correspondent

Usually as we age, we look back on those carefree (care*less?*) renegade days of youth and wish we had listened to our parents. Sure, I should have obeyed curfew more often, straightened up my junk drawer, and ditched that boy from the other side of the tracks just like Mom and Dad told me, but there's one area where I really wish I'd let my obstinate streak run free. That's in real estate.

Oh, the nest egg I would have now if I had spent my time fighting about mortgages instead of hemlines.

It was my senior year of college at Howard University in Washington, D.C. I had lived in various dormitories for my first three years, but as a soon-to-graduate upperclassman, I'd had enough of the kids and the noise in the dorms. I was almost grown, you know. What senior wants to be bothered with a bunch of childish sophomores and juniors—and forget about *freshmen*. Who wants a pack of those on your dorm floor?!

I looked longingly at the high-rise apartment buildings across the street from my dormitory on Washington's Sixteenth Street NW. To my twenty-year-old mind, the Dorchester was nine stories of elegance and sophistication. Or maybe the Washington House, with its high white walls and curved turrets, and those circular driveways—they *screamed* Sexy Single Sophisticate. So, against my parents' wishes, I rented a studio on a front corner of the Washington House. As far as I was concerned, $175 a month was a bargain for being able to breeze through the glass doors and be greeted by a cheery "Good evening, Miss Mabrey" from the very sweet Ethiopian receptionist. Never mind that my worldly air ended the second I stepped inside my apartment. There, I slept on a mattress atop a wooden pallet, and the rest of my furnishings consisted of a Huey Newton wicker chair and matching side table set in front of that fabled turret window.

My parents were appalled. They were worried—not only for my safety, but also because they feared that by moving off campus I was no longer having The College Experience. They urged me to give up my lease and move back to the dorm. It was a verbal tug-of-war, but with them in St. Louis and me a thousand miles away, it was a battle I could win. I stayed put.

Having tasted freedom, I wanted more. It was the 1970s. All over Washington, gracious old row houses and handsome apartment buildings in previously blighted neighborhoods were ripe for new life. One of those was a high-rise on Columbia Road called the Woodley, in the heart of the romantically named Adams-Morgan community. It was one of those graceful wedding cake buildings from much earlier in the century: I marveled at the brick- and stonework every time I passed by.

One day, a sign went up: the Woodley had been turned into condominiums! I could own my very own cosmopolitan plot. I stepped into the sales office and crunched the numbers. A studio was $19,000. One thousand down and my monthly payment would be $222. A one-bedroom could be had for $22,000.

I raced home and called my parents. Serendipitously, my grandparents down in Texas had just recently put $1,000 in a savings account for me. It was as if this was meant to be. Except they added my father's name to the account just to be sure I wouldn't fritter it away, one $3.99 tube of lipstick at a time. Let me have the thousand dollars to invest in an apartment, I begged my dad. It's only a few dollars more than I'm paying right now for rent, and it will appreciate, and when I need money later or I move away from Washington I can sell it, and I'll never ask you for another single thing as long as

I live, I swear. The answer was no. I'm sure I asked again. And possibly again after that, but the answer was always no.

I let it go. Can you believe it? After the years of defiance, all the arguments, the cajoling, the headstrong opposition—this time I just folded. Oh, I groused plenty to my friends. They heard about it every time we shared a five-dollar plate of Cuban chicken with black beans and rice at Omega, a restaurant across the street from the Woodley. They heard how I could have been living in luxury in my very own apartment, if only my parents had let me have *my very own* money.

And now, three decades later, I look in the classifieds and see a condo for sale in the Woodley. It's a one-bedroom, advertised as "one of the largest units," one that's "sunny," "open," and in a "fabulous building and location!" Lots of exclamation points marshal their way across the ad. And how much do they want for what I could have bought for $22,000 lo those many years ago? A mere $369,500—which they claim is $10,000 under market because it's for sale by owner.

Over the years, my father and I have been in the nation's capital together many times. We bemoan the loss of the Omega restaurant (okay, I bemoan its loss; he couldn't care less). We go to museums together, and remember the March on Washington and my childhood trips to the Smithsonian, and we both shake our heads at our foolish decision to let one of those Woodley condominiums slip through our hands.

I think about other real estate mistakes over the years, the relatives who've bought time-shares when we should have pooled our money and bought a beach house or condo. The huge old house I could have bought for $112,000 when I lived in Baltimore; it's now worth half a million. The London town house I rejected because I thought it was too large, opting instead for a tiny cottage . . . But I shouldn't complain—I didn't do too badly. The town house may have trebled in value, but my little cottage has almost doubled.

I tell my family about the neighbors who live across the hall from me in my Manhattan co-op—two sets of forward-thinking parents who bought apartments for their children attending college in New

York. They got them dirt cheap—probably $30,000 or $40,000—gracious old prewar two-bedroom apartments that sell today for three-quarters of a million dollars. And we realize that we all learned something.

What I Learned

If you're going to defy your parents, make it for something worthwhile. I look back at the pictures of myself with the big Angela Davis afro and the red velvet miniskirt and wonder what on earth I was thinking—and how my parents could have let me out of the house looking like *that*. But real estate? Buy something as soon as you possibly can. If you can afford it, when you're moving on up, buy your second, more spacious property, keep that first one and rent it out. Real estate is a long-term investment that usually—*not always*, but usually—appreciates. And getting on a solid financial footing as early in life as possible? That's worth fighting for.

STEVE SOMERS

Sports Talk Show Host

I wanted to say the biggest mistake in my life was taking up the tobacco.

Wrong.

Not quitting, not even wanting to, will be, as it probably is now, the biggest mistake in my life and the probable cause of my death . . .

I play Russian roulette with my life, eating right, exercising, then grabbing a smoke.

Lots of broccoli, lots of cigarettes. I believe that if it can happen to others, from Nat King Cole to Peter Jennings, it can probably happen to me.

I say "probably" because still in the back of your mind, you're hoping against hope it won't happen to you, and maybe it won't, and maybe that's just more denial. People say, "Hey, you're a smart guy. Why smoke?"

Well, I'm smart enough to know there are more things unknown to me than known, but there are choices and addictions, and as of this writing, I choose to be addicted, which I also think is not so smart.

It's like saying, "I'm in control of my addiction and choose to be that way, so mind your own business!" Also not so smart.

Smart is knowing that smoking can kill and socially and culturally makes you a "dirty and smelly outcast." Being charming or conversational, engaging, warm, or funny—all of this falls behind the social leper you've become, smoking away with all that firsthand smoke.

Sad that as I write this I have a cigarette burning nearby.

Don't breathe these words . . .

What I Learned

On the subject of smoking—sadly, so far nothing.

GORDON EDELSTEIN

Artistic Director, Long Wharf Theatre

The Ten Commandments are clear codes of behavior. We know when we have murdered someone, stolen something, or cheated on our spouse we have broken a commandment. But as adults in a complex grown-up world, we sometimes find that the line between right and wrong is not so clear. It is often at those times that we allow ourselves to cross that sometimes cloud-covered line.

One of the most important parts of my job as an artistic director of a theater is to go hunting. I sleep with one eye open, as I try to stay aware of what is exciting, fresh, and new in acting, directing, designing, and most of all playwriting. When I hear something move in the night, I chase it and try to bring it home to the Long Wharf Theatre. As I am never one to do something lightly, my pursuit can, at times, take on its own life. This is a story about one of those times and the ethical boundaries I crossed chasing a play and playwright I wanted. I will change the names of all the players in this story, but frankly, because I behaved badly, the name I would most like to change is my own.

I had become aware through the ever-active, multibranched theatrical grapevine of a very ambitious, large-scale play on religious and political themes that sounded like it would be very much to my taste. The play—lets call it *Pilgrimage*—is in three parts, and each part takes place in a different century. The playwright, Linda, was generating buzz around the country and in particular was receiving a great deal of attention from the Circle Theatre Company, one of our country's top regional theaters. It is run by Barbara Doyle, an old friend and colleague of mine. I have known Barbara since the mid-1980s, and we have always had a good deal of professional respect for each other and have had a warm relationship. Howard, Linda's agent, informed me that the Circle Theatre was developing *Pilgrimage* with Linda in residence, and that they were planning on putting together a reading of the entire play, and asked me if I would like to come. Howard told me that Barbara had not committed to producing the play and was encouraging my interest in it for Long Wharf, ours being a slightly more advantageous place to premiere a work because of its close proximity to New York. Howard was clearly coaxing me to hunt aggressively.

I called Barbara and told her of my enthusiasm for the play and I asked if I might come down to hear the reading. It became clear during my conversation with Barbara that she had worked closely and for some time with Linda on the play. Howard had underplayed her interest. Her excitement was palpable, and she expressed interest in co-producing the play with Long Wharf. I had real questions about co-producing *Pilgrimage* with Barbara for many reasons, primarily because I would have to sacrifice significant artistic control over the play, and because of its complexities, I was uncomfortable doing that. I was careful to parse my words but did not disabuse her of whatever assumptions she may have been making. It would have been better to make things clear at that moment, but I was avoiding a potentially uncomfortable conversation.

My trip to the Circle Theatre to hear the reading of *Pilgrimage* confirmed many things for me: (a) Linda's play was a massive undertaking, both expensive and risky, but potentially a thrilling night in the theater; (b) Barbara's commitment to this play was real and passionate; (c) either it was assumed that I wanted to co-produce the play with them or I was being heavily courted to do so. I was given a real VIP treatment at the Circle, which made me more uncomfortable. What were they assuming?

The next day I spoke with Linda's agent, who was pleased that my interest in the play continued, and he reiterated that Barbara's commitment to the play was not definite. He, as an agent, was not at all sure if the Circle even wanted to produce the play, or that he would grant them exclusive rights. In other words, he was suggesting that Long Wharf still might be able to produce it on its own in the next season and possibly have it moved to New York, leaving the Circle out.

The agent was very enthusiastic, and he encouraged me to call the playwright, Linda, and talk to her. It was at this point that I began to ignore my inner ethical alarm. It felt wrong somehow to go behind Barbara's back and compete for the play, but I avoided real reflection on the matter, and when inner objections would rise up in me, I justified my actions by telling myself that it is a dog-eat-dog world and I was just competing for something that was up for grabs. I work for Long Wharf, and it is my job to secure the best and most important material that I can.

The honorable next step would have been to call Barbara and tell her that although I respected her emotional and artistic involvement in the play and appreciated all the work she had done with Linda, I was not interested in pursuing a co-production with her. I ought to have asked her if she was indeed committed to do the play without me, and if she was, I should have had a candid conversation with her about my interest in pursuing the play without her. Technically she did not have exclusive rights to the play, but I would probably not be pursuing the play without her work on it. The right thing to do would have been to let her have the first shot at it and see if she could generate enough interest in it herself to give it a future.

But I didn't do that. I chose to believe Howard, the agent, and not my eyes and ears. I said to myself that Barbara had not made her definitive move on the play so it was anyone's project to pursue.

The next day I called Linda and took her to lunch. She is a charming and smart woman but a relative neophyte in the business of the theater. She was pleased to be courted so aggressively, and I asked her if she would be interested in my trying to set up a production that would begin at Long Wharf and move to New York. Linda was thrilled at the opportunity without fully understanding—I believe—the ramifications for the Circle, and she gave me permission to pursue this option. In my heart I knew I was doing something smarmy—not clearly wrong, but I was doing something to Barbara that I would not want someone to do to me. That may be the final barometer to measure ethical behavior: How would I feel if someone else behaved as I was behaving?

As time went on I was feeling worse and worse about what I had done. I struggled with guilt over my behavior, but I still refused to admit to myself that I had let my type A–style aggression drown my ethical knowledge. Barbara learned of my lunch with Linda, and as much as I hated doing it, I felt as though I had to call her. Haltingly I told Barbara that I did not want to produce the play with her, and that if I did it, I wanted to do it by myself. She said, "Stop right there. You know, I am having some real problems with the ethics of your behavior here." I had been caught, and I had nothing to say. I fumbled some sort of apology with broken sentences and long pauses and then got off the phone, deciding not to pursue the play any further. In a feeble attempt to apologize again, I sent her a bouquet of flowers on her opening night of *Pilgrimage*. The play ran at the Circle and is now being considered for production at other prominent theaters around the country.

My sense of shame is so great that I no longer pursue *Pilgrimage* even though I would not be in competition with the Circle anymore. The project for me is a vivid reminder of behavior of which I am ashamed. I have seen Barbara a number of times in professional settings, and it is awkward between us; I am sure that she feels betrayed and hurt.

WHAT I LEARNED

It is so easy to talk yourself out of an ethical decision, especially when you are going to directly benefit from your unethical behavior. When the situation is complex and the line between right and wrong is obscured, the only way I know to figure out the "right thing to do" is to try to listen to the voice inside me and remember that we should do unto others as we would have them do unto us. The late Christopher Reeve was fond of quoting Abraham Lincoln: "When I do good, I feel good; when I do bad, I feel bad, and that is my religion." Words to live by.

BOB SHAYE

Co-Chairman and Co-CEO, New Line Cinema

I was doing pretty damn well. I had started my company, with three thousand dollars, out of a fifth-floor walk-up in the Village.

It wasn't easy. There was much adversity, but with hard work we prospered.

Our films began to click with the public. Our earnings rose year after year. Drexel Burnham took us public. I was the largest shareholder of a successful publicly traded organization.

My personal net worth began to skyrocket. Sure, I'd earned every penny, and sure, it was fun, and I was getting bloody rich, and prideful.

Then Ted Turner proposed a merger. I grew to really like Ted. I got to know him pretty well and trusted him, as he trusted me. I was on his board. Now I was the second largest individual shareholder of Ted's company. I had full autonomy, a lot more capital to deploy in filmmaking, and it was still my company, or so it seemed.

Then Turner was bought by Time Warner. I wasn't invited to join their board, but I held on to this new version of my equity, as if New Line were still my company, and that stock increased in value. Not that our company's success made it go up or down, but I was worth hundreds of millions. "My" company was doing just fine.

Then senior management decided to merge with an Internet company. It was called a merger, but it was a sellout. Disaster of every possible nature befell this new entity. The stock plunged. My net worth plunged.

The faith ultimately placed in the hands of strangers became a disaster for us all. By anyone's standards, I'm still in very fine shape, but 90 percent of one's net worth is a lot to lose.

What I Learned

There was a moment I should have realized that my company was no longer mine. Loyalty is a noble emotion, but it must be applied with reason and insight and caution. As someone said, "The price of freedom is eternal vigilance." It's not smart to both sell and keep. I had sold my control. I should have sold my stock.

JANE ROSENTHAL

Partner and Cofounder, Tribeca Productions, Tribeca Film Festival

I have always been one of those people who get quite nauseous on roller-coaster rides, so I try to avoid them like the plague, but it is now clear to me that I have picked a career in the wrong industry. And the summer and fall of 2000 certainly made this clear to me. For as Dickens said, "It was the best of times, it was the worst of times."

Let me tell you a little bit about those ninety days. The lowest of the low occurred on opening weekend in June for a film I had spent seven years developing. With much fanfare and anticipation *Rocky and Bullwinkle* came to the silver screen one Friday afternoon. By the five o'clock show we were in full cardiac arrest, by the nine o'clock show rigor mortis had set in, and by Saturday morning, we were sitting shiva. However, I did discover a little-known Jewish custom for the film business: out of respect for the dead, no one, and I mean no one, calls for a full seventy-two hours. The silence of a bomb is deafening.

My husband, Craig, put it best: "I guess they don't know what to say!" And you really haven't experienced life (to its fullest) until you've read over breakfast an entire article in the *Wall Street Journal* on how your "doozy" of a project got made in the first place. What I had intended as a smart and funny love letter to childhood icons in a market desperately in need of alternative family entertainment just didn't work.

And then, like magic, it was suddenly the best of times. Just a few short months later, another film I produced, *Meet the Parents*, opened to glowing reviews and a record box office. I can now speak with great confidence from my personal experience that (not surprisingly) good times are much more fun. I also learned something important along the way.

WHAT I LEARNED

The euphoria from a big hit is fleeting, but the sense of personal loss and devastation that comes from a labor of love gone bad is everlasting. As the years have passed, I have come to realize that we learn as much, if not more, about ourselves from our failures as we learn from our successes. As filmmakers we must be willing to take the risk and buy an all-day ticket on that virtual roller-coaster ride we call filmmaking, even if it sometimes makes us nauseous, because as someone once said, "This too will pass." And it just comes with the territory.

BOBBY VALENTINE

Former Baseball Manager, New York Mets, and Current Manager, Chiba Lotte Marines, Japan

I was in college in 1971. I had just finished playing a season of baseball for Tommy Lasorda in Washington with the Spokane Indians. I was the shortstop for the championship AAA team and the MVP of the league, and I was twenty years old. I led the league in seven different categories and won the batting title.

We played a playoff series between the winners of the East, the Indians, and the winners of the West, the Hawaii Islanders. The series started in Spokane, and we won the first two games easily at our home ballpark. We went to Hawaii to continue the best of seven series. I was booed when I took the field because I'd beat out a fine experienced hitter, Winston Llanas, for the batting title on the last day of the regular season by getting three hits in the game. The two hundred and eleventh hit of the season for me was a ball I hit to third, which could have gone for a hit or an error, but our hometown scorer ruled it a hit. A lot was written about the call and not much about the other two hundred and ten hits, so when I got to the island many of the loyal Hawaii Islanders fans made it clear they were not very happy to see me.

We won the game and I got three hits, including a home run. I was even cheered by their home crowd. I was the leadoff hitter for game four, just as I was for every game of the 1970 season, and the pitcher, Greg Washburne, hit me with the first pitch of the game. As I fell away from the plate, the ball followed me and landed with its full force on my left cheekbone. My face collapsed immediately, and within an hour I was in the ER of the hospital, ready for an operation to pull my cheekbone back up three and a half inches to its normal position.

In 1971 the United States still had a military draft, and if you were not crazy, handicapped, married with kids, or a full-time student, you were off to Vietnam. I had been a full-time student at the University of Southern California the year before and intended to return, but while I was in the hospital the team I belonged to, the Los Angeles Dodgers, had pulled some strings and enrolled me in Arizona State University in Tempe, near where the Dodgers had a training camp.

At the end of the 1970 season I was the heir apparent to Maury Wills, the shortstop with the Dodgers. After winning just about everything I could, and playing all the games, it seemed that I would be given the job the next year in Los Angeles, but I was not around for the September call-up. My head was bandaged for about two weeks, and the team was not going to commit to me, as they didn't know how I would react as a hitter after the beaning. I was enrolled in Arizona State University when the doctor gave me the okay to play in the Arizona Instructional League, where the Dodgers had a team just down the road from Arizona State, in Mesa.

No one was happier than I was to play and show the top men I could still do the job. I was off to the games in the Instructional League. I passed all the tests of playing and got my hits and proved that I was not going to let a little ball to the face stand in my way. Classes continued, and when the military draft lottery was established my number was in the high three hundreds. I really felt blessed.

I was living in the Sigma Chi fraternity house and was enjoying time as a student and a player with a few bucks in his pocket. The house had a flag football team. Flag football is a version of American football, but instead of tackling players, the defensive team must remove a flag or flag belt from the ball carrier. Over the years, contact leagues have emerged, in which offensive and defensive players can block in certain zones.

We had a bunch of great jocks who would get together and have fun on the field and fun after the game as well. We were undefeated going into the last game of the season. It was two weeks from spring training and the semester was winding down. The final flag football game was against the law school team. We'd shut them out the week before, and I really didn't see any reason to play them again. I woke up the morning of the game and had dreamed that rain had canceled the game, but we were in Arizona and this was not the case. I had a strong feeling in my gut that I should not play this game. There was nothing in it. I had already proven to most that my speed and agility were not to be matched on the ASU flag football field. But after talking to the guys I decided to start the game and just be a decoy for the other guys and let everyone else have the fun.

Well, on the opening kickoff I was the decoy as we faked a reverse with me pretending to get a handoff. I made my fake and my teammate ran down the sideline as I watched the other team try to get his flag. While I was watching, somehow I was clipped from the side and my knee was torn apart. I tried to tell the Dodgers that this happened practicing baseball, but it didn't matter. I went to the most important spring training of my life in a full leg cast. When I was finally able to run full speed again, Maury Wills had resigned from the Dodgers, but they began grooming Bill Russell to be the shortstop.

What I Learned

I knew that day to trust my gut, but I didn't have the courage to tell my peers that I had "a feeling." Since that day I have always tried to trust my gut. There were times when the results were not perfect, but I always know that the right way to go is with what you feel is right.

HENRY S. SCHLEIFF

CEO, Hallmark Network

I am lucky to have some very good friends and even more fortunate to have a friend like Chuck Grodin, who's constantly doing favors for others, including myself, and asking for nothing in return. This is why I am writing this brief note about mistakes—and what I have learned from them. At first glance, you might not see the connection, but hopefully the following will clear that up. You see, Chuck Grodin is one of the most successful and creative people in the industry—he's a writer, producer, actor (film, TV, and theater), TV host, and syndicated radio commentator, and he's probably taken on a few roles I've omitted. He asked some of his friends to submit their thoughts on mistakes and what they have learned. As usual with Chuck, it's for a good cause: all of his proceeds from the sale of this book will go to HELP USA, which provides a variety of critical services to the less fortunate, such as low-cost housing, job opportunities, and the like. And, as you can see from the list of people who have contributed pieces for this book, many of Chuck's friends and colleagues have answered his call, not only because it is a rare favor that he has asked of them but because of the relief to so many that this book will help provide. Chuck asked me more than once to contribute, and I didn't say no. But since I am so busy, as most of us are, I never really responded, which is even more egregious because I'm a fellow board member of Chuck's for HELP USA.

My mistake was that I hadn't responded to a minor request, for a noble purpose, from someone who has given so much to me, my family, and, indeed, our society with his successful advocacy for prison reform and his efforts on behalf of the homeless. While I was trying to think of what my biggest mistake is, my most important mistake—and, believe me, the volume is staggering—I realized my most recent mistake. I should have understood that a dear friend was asking for a favor, not even on his behalf but rather to benefit an important organization like HELP USA.

What I Learned

I've learned that sometimes you have to see the bigger picture—that is, as busy as we all are, we should be quicker to respond to a friend, especially one who is so interested in helping others. Anyway, I'm glad I've contributed these few words—I'm glad I caught this mistake and rectified it, in my fashion, before it was too late.

Most of all, I can't wait for another friend who is trying to help people to ask me for something. And, Chuck, if you have another book, just give me a call—but if it's on mistakes, I'll have to find another one!

KHALIAH ALI
AS TOLD TO LAWRENCE LINDNER

President, Khaliah Ali Apparel

My son's school was going to hold an auction to raise money for scholarships. I promised to get sports stars to contribute memorabilia—boxing gloves from various fights, basketball jerseys, and so on. I promised I would get figures in fashion to donate items like pocketbooks, front-row seats to shows, and other auctionable items. I promised too that I'd help with media planning, and also promised to help with planning the nuts and bolts of the event itself. I promised myself way into overcommitment. Everything I said I would do was on top of my already overextended workload—running my clothing line and going to bat for a number of other charities, not to mention raising my son.

I handled the pressure in what seemed at the time to be the best approach. I procrastinated. "I have three more months" became "I have two more months" became "I still have three weeks," and then reality hit.

In the end, I managed to pull off somewhere between 50 and 70 percent of what I had said I could accomplish. It wasn't a complete disaster, but in the process, I made people at the school really nervous, and also put them out because they had to go the extra mile as a result of my own lack of punctuality and get things to the auction that I had said I would get there myself. A lot of the items came in literally moments before the auctioneer started talking.

Everyone was very gracious, and even grateful for my contributions, but that only made it worse. I knew I had let them down and caused a lot of anxiety and drama that just hadn't been necessary.

I let myself down too. I love my son's school and all that it does for him and really wanted to give back. But something that should have been a joyful endeavor became a miserable chore because I had let things slide. It all turned into an obligation rather than something coming from a willing place.

What I Learned

You owe people your authenticity. The truth was that I could never have possibly come through on everything I had promised, and although I meant well, if I had followed the principle of truth up front, it would have made everything very easy. There's a natural law and order in the world, and things flow if you just follow it. In this particular case, if I had promised less and delivered 100 percent of what I promised, it would have gone a lot further than my promising more but not being able to deliver the whole package.

I also learned that love is a gift, not an obligation. If you remain true to yourself and do what's really doable rather than promise too much because you think you're supposed to, the gift of love you have to offer will remain true.

JOHN BURTON

California State Senator, 1997–2005

W hen I was going to law school I worked as a bartender at Bimbo's 365 nightclub, and a friend of mine, Michael O'Neil, and I were as close to being degenerate gamblers as kids in their twenties could be. One day Mike came to me and said, "Bernard (which, God only knows why, was his favorite nickname for me), I've got an immortal lock."

The Cleveland Browns football team, which was a powerhouse in those days, was playing the San Francisco 49ers in San Francisco that Sunday in an exhibition game. Mike said, "The Browns are only laying six points. It's an absolute lock—let's scrape up money and bet the house." In those days the house would have been two hundred dollars each. We had trouble finding a bookmaker to take the bet and chased all over town trying to get it down. Finally, five minutes before game time, we found a part-time bookie sitting in the Lucky Club, a bar on Stanyan and Haight near Kezar Stadium. We joyfully laid the bet and gave him our two hundred each, then went to watch the game. The 49ers ended up beating the Browns, and we lost our money. As we were leaving the game, somewhat pissed off, one of our buddies asked why we would ever bet on the Browns in an exhibition game when it was common knowledge that Paul Brown, Cleveland's coach, never cared about winning exhibitions.

WHAT I LEARNED

Never bet on a Paul Brown team during the exhibition season, but more important, never go around chasing an immortal lock bet, because whenever you do, the odds are that you'll lose. I have learned many other things from my many mistakes in life, but for some odd reason that is the one that I always remember.

PHIL MILLER, MD, FACS

Facial Plastic Surgeon

In the beginning of my surgical training, a well-respected, illustrious, and talented surgeon stood in front of our class of surgical interns and said, "An excellent surgeon is not one who is technically skilled. An excellent surgeon is one who is truly gifted, one who has that unique ability to determine when to perform those techniques and when not to, when to operate and when not to operate, and when to do certain maneuvers and when not to do certain maneuvers. That is a truly gifted and excellent surgeon."

Those were the words that inspired me during my surgical training. Through the long and arduous process, the endless sleepless nights, the demanding pace and pressure, I tried to never forget those words of wisdom. There is a lot to learn in becoming a surgeon, and I wondered when the time would come, if ever, that I would be granted that gift presented by my first mentor.

Throughout the years, after thousands of operations that I first witnessed, then assisted in, then performed, the technical skills came and the intended results followed. The prodigious information was transformed to knowledge and then second nature, and, finally, consistent and reliable results were obtained. But I among many of my colleagues strove for true excellence. And so, though I found my patients increasingly satisfied with their results, I have been somewhat irked by results that could have been slightly better.

I went back to the books; I learned and studied more; I began reading more what others had conceived and thought. Nevertheless, the results again were satisfying the patients but not satisfying me. No matter what I tried, no matter what I read, no matter what I heard, I was incapable of bringing my results to that next level.

One day while in the operating room performing a delicate maneuver on the tip of a patient's nose, I heard myself telling myself to do a maneuver that I had not considered until that very moment. It was a feeling that I had experienced countless times in the operating room but had always ignored. Instead, I would always follow the well-thought-out, meticulous, and comprehensive plan that I had orchestrated. Once again my initial response was to ignore that thought. But then it dawned on me: nothing else had worked; nothing else had been able to elevate my results to a greater place. And so, carefully and with some trepidation, I followed my instinct and performed the maneuver. And the moment I completed it, like a lightning bolt it struck me that this quiet voice, this intuitive sense acquired after years and years of training, was the answer to the problem. I performed that minor adjustment, and lo and behold, the end result was spectacular. I had achieved the insight and used the gift my mentor had referred to years ago.

What I Learned

Although there is no substitute for thorough preparation for any initiative, you must be open to a spontaneous intuitive sense telling you to take a different direction. This intuitive sense is distinct from anxious fear or a debilitating insecurity. Rather, it stems from an experienced and confident knowledge that a subtle modification, or an alteration, or perhaps even an entirely different path could render extraordinary results.

ERVIN DRAKE

Songwriter, "It Was a Very Good Year" and "I Believe"

I made a major career mistake by forming a songwriting partnership with a man named Jimmy. He was ten years older than I and had a different frame of reference in the pop arts, since he had come of age in the Al Jolson generation and I was pure Crosby/Sinatra. We had veto power on what we should write. I chose an older partner because I had always composed songs of the kind written by my idols: Porter, Rodgers/Hart, Kern/Hammerstein, Arlen/Harburg. I felt I could not write the commercial kind of Tin Pan Alley song, and I deeply wanted to make my livelihood in that field. Well, Jimmy could sure as hell write commercially or a switch on "what had been written before." In other words, derivative work that was never fresh. Therefore, year after year we wrote very tired lyrics and melodies.

Jimmy was a confirmed bachelor who stayed out late every night of the week and would show up at our office in the Brill Building any time he woke up, sometimes arriving at one p.m., just in time for lunch. To a married man with children who was trying to pursue a meaningful career, this was terribly defeating, and at times angered me. I let him know it from time to time, and he would shape up—for a while. Then too I wanted to write a Broadway musical comedy. That had always been my ultimate target. I felt I could function at my best in that area, but Jimmy refused to write anything of that magnitude "on spec."

It wasn't until after we wrote "I Believe (For Every Drop of Rain

That Falls . . .)" that I realized my profound mistake. When we created the song for a TV series, Jimmy pointed out that the musical structure I outlined was not the structure that Meredith Wilson had chosen for his song of faith, "May the Good Lord Bless and Keep You." Once again he was looking for a paradigm that we might emulate with a slight switch. I answered that this song was just for a TV show, over and out, and therefore, why not do anything we felt like? That logic won him over, and "I Believe" became one of the biggest worldwide hits I've ever had. I then made up my mind that the next time I wrote a song of that potential magnitude, I would do it all alone, influenced by no one's veto but my own, and that came about when I composed "It Was a Very Good Year." I never could have written this song while I was collaborating with Jimmy. And then I wrote the score to *What Makes Sammy Run?*

Before breaking our partnership, I asked my wife's opinion. We were both very fond of Jimmy, and for good reason. He was a thoroughly decent, honest man whom our kids called uncle. I told Ada that I feared that if I split with him he would sink without a trace in our business—both in songs and television employment. She said that as fond as she was of him, the most important consideration was how I felt about myself in my work. She knew of my deep frustration over the years of never being able to accomplish my aims. Jimmy and I split, and as I feared, he sank without a trace.

It was not all that easy for me. When I told my agent, the William Morris Office, that I wanted single representation, they replied that I had "no track record as a single" and asked if I would just continue to let them offer me with Jimmy. "No," I answered. I asked for and received my authorization papers back.

WHAT I LEARNED

Since then I have followed my own inner polar star. I still listen to thoughts that differ from mine, but I am more careful in what I accept.

PEGGY SIEGAL

Public Relations Executive

For the past twenty-five years my career has evolved from working on national publicity campaigns to running projects for all types of motion pictures to specializing in very specific VIP screenings and media positioning of films. If you still have no idea what I do, neither does anyone else, so I always say, "I'm in catering" and "I went to college to be an usher."

I have developed a database of 20,000 accomplished people, coded by occupation. When my company is hired to screen a film prior to release, we are able to devise a list exactly tailored for those who will respond favorably—I hope—and spread the word.

A few years ago, before my life-changing business collaboration with Bryan Bantry, I was asked by Lorne Michaels to organize a New York screening of his new film, *Mean Girls*. The movie was highly anticipated because it starred the hottest teen actress in the country, Lindsay Lohan. Paramount Pictures had made it very clear that this event was a "favor" to Lorne because he lives in New York and they were spending a fortune on a Los Angeles premiere. I have been a huge fan of Lorne's since the beginning of *Saturday Night Live*. Being very precise, he was not easy to work for. So working with Allison Jackson, the special-events person at the studio, I began to put the night together. Paramount chose the brand-new Time Warner lobby, not the coziest place for a teen party. We hired designer David Monn, and in addition, I insisted we bring in the "bar mitzvah king of New York," Tom Kaufman, to create the ultimate teen happening, complete with makeup counters, enormous Polaroids, a make-your-own-CD booth, and karaoke . . . all approved by Lorne.

We put together the perfect list, mostly famous friends of Lorne's and their kids. The Lohan family was given approximately twenty-five seats. As the RSVPs started coming in, I noticed that the Lohan family, specifically Lindsay's father, had invited half of Long Island. He eventually went to jail, but not for sabotaging his own daughter's event . . . which in my book of justice remains his biggest crime today. Allison Jackson was powerless to control Lindsay's dad. I begged for another screening room, which the studio would not provide.

The night of the "special screening" arrived, and an executive from Paramount, who had just gotten his prestigious job a week before, flew in with a companion and another couple. We were severely overbooked and I saw the writing on the wall. The entire theater was packed and every seat was filled with celebrities like Jimmy Buffett, Caroline Kennedy, James Gandolfini, and NBC family members Jimmy Fallon, Tina Fey, Brian Williams, and Dick Ebersol. In a moment of profound confusion, and in hindsight, the dumbest decision I ever made, I asked the newly appointed Paramount executive to get up and give his four seats to latecomer Dan Aykroyd and his family. Why would I humiliate the very people who pay my bills? Because it was Lorne's screening for his friends and Dan Aykroyd was an original cast member of *SNL*. This snap decision haunts me to this day. The executive, who is one of the nicest guys I know from Miramax, took his friends out to dinner. Little did I know the extent of his hurt feelings and the revenge of his PR staff.

The film and party were both smashes. Lorne got calls the next day from all the greats and near-greats.

The Paramount PR people began to plot my assassination. I got wind of the first blow from Richard Johnson, editor of the *New York Post*'s lethal "Page Six." I tried to defend myself in print, which was a joke. I called every member of Paramount's PR staff to personally apologize. I sent flowers everywhere. I sent champagne to the executive. I whined and cried all over town. I phoned other studio heads to see if I had made the wrong call; they laughed at me and said I had done the right thing. Apparently not, however, by Paramount's standards. More nasty column items continued to run. I flew to Los Angeles to personally apologize and people refused to see me.

Two years later an editor at "Page Six" wrote a book reprinting the whole mess and editorializing that although I worked very hard and did a great job, my people skills, or lack thereof, left me washed-up and dead. It was a nightmare that wouldn't go away. Every studio in Hollywood knew Paramount would never work with me again.

Years later, my producer friend of twenty-five years, Paramount's Michael Shamberg, whom I'd met on the set of *The Big Chill*, tried to hire me on *World Trade Center*. The doors at Paramount were still locked. It was just amazing how *Mean Girls* continued to haunt me.

What I Learned

Do I now know who I work for? Have I become a little more empathetic to people's feelings in an overbooked theater? You bet. Do I continue to have seating crises? You bet. But now I keep everyone very calm. By the end of 2006, the woman who caused me so much grief was gone. Finally I was hired to do special screenings on *World Trade Center* and *Babel*, and I'd learned to always have an extra chair.

ART GARFUNKEL

Singer-Songwriter

Now that I look back on it, my mistake seems like an alpine peak of folly—the Matterhorn of madness. Maybe we find our ways to these heights of spectacular stupidity by patient increments, ever loyal to the climb.

It was sometime in 1968. We were mixing "Mrs. Robinson," Paul and Roy Halee and I. This means we were in a control room of a recording studio, Columbia's, at the soundboard, locking in the relationships of thirty-two channels of music, with our six hands. We worked through the night against a morning deadline—a sold-out tour awaited. The first show was the very next night—big show, the Jungfrau!

I guess I first started playing on elevated ground in the recording studio in my high school years. In my college years when Simon and Garfunkel hit, I was propelled into American business, having serious fun making records, trying to keep a perspective. So a show gets booked on Yom Kippur night near home, and you honor the gig— this is *not carried away by fame*.

Through the late 1960s—through albums, concerts, and *The Graduate*, I stayed focused on the fun at hand, and pretty unfocused on many other things. Now we were coming to the end of recording the *Bookends* album. The artwork was done, credits and packaging complete, ready to ship, waiting only for Paul and Artie to finish the last drop, "Mrs. Robinson." The studio phone rings at midnight:

"They're sending over a union rep to bust you guys for manually sharing in your recording engineer's work." We put our spy at the elevator while we nervously mixed against the clock.

Maybe it was six-thirty a.m. when we finished "Mrs. R." *Bookends* was now done. I went home to my New York apartment for a little bit of sleep before the last flight to our first sold-out appearance for the album tour. My deep satisfaction led to a deep sleep. I slept through the alarm and the flight! There was no show! Thousands of people were sent home disappointed.

What I Learned

Don't let deep satisfaction infringe on deep responsibilities.

ARLENE ALDA

Children's Book Author,
Photographer

Life magazine—*the* magazine for good photography—had given me an important assignment, and it meant a lot to me. I got to the New York offices first thing in the morning after having flown all night from Los Angeles on the red-eye. I was going to meet my deadline just in time. The year was 1983.

I had spent an exhilarating week of practically nonstop photography of the last days of the TV show *M*A*S*H*. The results of the shoot would appear in the magazine—in color—with my byline. What a coup. I had no illusions about why they had chosen me, even though I was a published photographer. One of the editors had seen a book that I had photographed and written, and he saw that I was okay. I could do a good job. But it didn't hurt, either, that I was the wife of the lead actor in the show, Alan Alda, and I had that magic ticket called "access." It didn't bother me that I had been picked because of that. I knew that I could deliver, given the chance. I worked harder than ever to cover everything that I felt would give the viewer a good idea of what it was like that last week, behind the scenes, on that fabled set. What I didn't realize was that I would be exhausted from the overnight flight and that without sleep I couldn't even think straight.

I handed over about two hundred slides that I had culled during the week, from about a thousand or more. The editor in chief immediately went over to a light box and began reviewing the slides. He got them down to enough for what he said would be a six-page spread. My heart was beating fast from excitement, even through that haze of sleepiness and jet lag.

When I asked to see what he selected, my bubble burst. I stared at the pictures in silence. One of the shots, which he wanted as a double-page spread, was out of focus. "Please don't use that shot," I pleaded. "I have another of the same scene, shot a fraction of a second later, that is *in* focus. That's the one I meant to give you."

I counted two mistakes at the same time: (1) I gave him the wrong picture, and (2) I was begging.

The editor in chief seemed unmoved, especially by my begging. He was in a hurry. I was almost in tears. Why would he use a slightly out-of-focus shot when I had one that was in focus? I guess his ego wasn't at stake the way mine seemed to be and he wasn't bothered by the photo the way I was.

Another editor took me aside and said in a kind manner, "*Show* him your other slide. Don't just ask. He has no time to look for it. *You* look for it." I awakened from my self-pity and went over to a light box. I went through boxes of slides. I knew that I had the photo . . . but where? After what seemed like forever, I finally found it. I presented it to the editor in chief. "This is the shot that I meant to give you, instead of the out-of-focus one," I said. He took it, looked at it, and said "Okay." As simple as that. Why had I assumed that I had no power when I really had a solution? Was it sheer exhaustion? Politeness? I had felt helpless. What an awful feeling, and I didn't need to feel that way.

WHAT I LEARNED

It's taken me much of my adult life to realize that respect for others doesn't mean that I have to put my own good sense aside. Most of us have more options than we think we have. That session at *Life* magazine made a powerful impression on me. Don't complain. Do something about it. Be proactive . . . Yes! Of course, taking the right actions is one of life's ongoing challenges. It feels so much better to find solutions than to slip into helpless/complaining mode.

JAMES M. NEDERLANDER

Theater Owner

Many years ago the Uris Building, which was a large office building in New York that was also the home of the Uris Theatre, was for sale. The people who owned it had declared bankruptcy, and I could have bought it by simply taking over the mortgage payments, but I was a theater owner and I didn't want to be in the business of renting office space, so I declined. Today that building, which is also the home of the Gershwin Theatre on Broadway, is worth an incredible fortune.

What I Learned

I was crazy. Sometimes when an opportunity presents itself, you should just take that unexpected turn in the road.

MORT ZUCKERMAN

Owner, *U.S. News and World Report* and the *New York Daily News*

As I look back on my life and think about what my biggest mistake was, there is a long list from which I could make a selection. One that I chose is my failure to take music lessons. I would love to be able to play the piano or cello or anything that would enable me to lose myself to music. I started to take piano lessons in Boston before I moved to New York, and once I moved here I lost the teacher and the impetus.

WHAT I LEARNED

Thus, I remain shy of any musical abilities and greatly regret it.

HOWARD J. RUBENSTEIN

President, Rubenstein Associates, Inc.

After graduating from the University of Pennsylvania, Phi Beta Kappa and third in my class, I entered Harvard Law School. I went there at the insistence of my mother and father, who wanted me to be a lawyer or a judge. After two months, I quit. I didn't want to be a lawyer—I didn't think that I liked or wanted to do it as a profession. I went home to Brooklyn, untrained for anything. My parents thought I was making a big mistake.

My father, looking to steer me in the right direction, encouraged me to go into public relations, and I got one small account—an old-age home. It paid me one hundred dollars a month and I worked from my mother's kitchen table, using a portable typewriter. I pecked away and wrote some stories. I then asked my mother to answer the phone "Howard J. Rubenstein Associates," and she refused. She, in turn, basically kicked me out of the house. That was the beginning of my career.

But after three or four years, I still didn't feel I had a profession. Back then, public relations was looked down on. Many people thought that PR people were just snake oil salesmen with a complete lack of professionalism. I was concerned I'd made a tremendous mistake, and I went back to law school at night, finishing St. John's University School of Law in four years and first in my class. Although I was offered a number of jobs in law, including assistant counsel to the House Judiciary Committee, I ultimately determined that I enjoyed PR and committed to making a career of it.

So in reality, what I thought was a tremendous mistake in leaving Harvard ended up being the best "mistake" I could have made. When I went back to finish my law degree, I found I was more focused and better able to appreciate the value of my education. I believe my law degree has served me extremely well in the public relations business.

What I Learned

Do what you want to do in love and in your profession. Appreciate the value of a good education. You have to work very hard at everything. What appears to be a mistake is sometimes a blessing—that's what I've found.

ROBERT REDFORD

Academy Award–Winning Actor, Director

I grew up in a lower-working-class neighborhood in southwest Los Angeles, and there wasn't much available entertainment. It was the middle of World War II, and aside from a Saturday-night walk to a neighborhood movie house and a midweek trip to the library to check out something from the children's section (Rafael Sebastian was big), you were pretty much on your own. You were the entertainment that you created.

I decided to face the monotony of everyday chores and humdrum tasks by making them a game. I'd climb and count stairs after guessing how many. I'd watch a car moving into an intersection and would take odds on the green turning yellow. I'd count steps to the corner. And so on.

As I grew older and more adventure and movement came my way, I still maintained this notion of making a game out of any boring repetitive ritual. I'd turn jobs that were mostly common labor into creative, challenging contests to be won—routines to be cut short and tricked.

At the Standard Oil Refinery (now Chevron) in El Segundo, California, I secured a job as a roustabout in the oil fields. By angling and cajoling, I advanced to the chemical waste department, where I was a bottle washer. My father was an accountant in the accounting department high above in the same building. He was lucky to have secured this job, which he would have for life, when the Great Depression spilled into the Second World War.

I was lazy. I wanted something more challenging than sweating and grunting for eight hours, lifting lifeless, heavy objects in the jack-hammering noise of teeth-rattling drills plunging into hot wasted concrete. So shortly after landing a cushier but no less boring job putting bottles on spigots in a revolving cistern, I got antsy and inventive. When a complete cycle of bottles finished making their rounds in the washing machine, another worker would load the six to eight twelve-quart bottles into cases, stack the cases on a cart with a dolly handle, wheel them into an elevator, take them up to the loading dock, wheel them out to the edge, and stop, unhook the cart from the dolly, and leave it there for trucks, which would back into the loading zone and load them.

To keep this task interesting, I began to improvise. I would add extra cases to the load, then get fancy wheeling the cart into the elevator and out onto the loading dock, going faster each time to try to beat the time spent, then run the cart up to the guard block at the edge of the dock and yank the dolly handle out of the slot all in one motion, then race back down and check my time.

One day the extra weight on the car made the load too top-heavy, and the sudden stop overran the guard block and the entire load tipped out of my grasp and cascaded down into the street in a cacophony of crashing, breaking bottles. All of them. It sounded like an incredible traffic accident, the din reverberating through the entire building and loading area. All the windows from the administration offices flew open in a panicked synchronicity to see me standing there above the rubble, a limp dolly handle in my hand, and in one of the windows was the face of my father—seeing his stature diminished by his irresponsible son.

It was not my first offense by trying to make my job more creative. I had been removed from other departments for similar escapades. I was fired—told to seek other employment elsewhere. My father kept his job but didn't speak to me for days, and he may have sought therapy for what mistakes were made in my upbringing. I was indeed humbled and chagrined.

WHAT I LEARNED

Despite my failure and hubris, the creative process does have virtue.

LILY TOMLIN

All-Around Charming Entertainer

So many mistakes rush to mind that I feel like a "star" about to implode. When I think of all the mistakes I've made, I realize that I'm the perfect person to contribute to this book.

My biggest mistake was the lack of courage I showed back in 1987.

Remember when Cher wore that dress to the Oscars in 1986? The dress was midriff-bare and there was a feather headdress? If you saw her in it, you've never forgotten it.

Well, I was going to wear that dress the next year. Cher was going to loan it to me, and we both thought it would be really funny. There was, however, one hitch: at the time, I was playing at the Kennedy Center and I would have to cancel two or three shows to go to the Oscars. So my publicist and the people at the Kennedy Center did everything they could to talk me out of it. They said people would think I was making fun of Cher, and I was being "indulgent and unfair" to people who would be disappointed when my shows were canceled at the Kennedy Center.

So, I didn't do it; I didn't wear that iconic dress to the Oscars and I didn't give my fans one of the most enjoyable and hilarious experiences of our lives together.

Of course, not everyone would've seen the humor. But to my hard-core fans (and you all know who you are), the moment would've been enough to bind us forever.

They wouldn't be asking about Ernestine or Edith Ann anymore; they wouldn't be snorting or fingering the insides of their shirts or blowing raspberries in theater lobbies or pushing shopping carts down the aisles.

They'd say, "You know, when she wore Cher's dress on the Oscars, we laughed our asses off; we fell off the couch, and we couldn't take our eyes off the TV. Every time the camera moved, we screamed, 'Give us another shot of Lily and the dress!'"

I can just hear them, fans all over the world: "That was the one time, Lily, that my husband and I—and the kids—got together, and we could watch something that we all got a kick out of, all of us laughing at the same time. It brought us together, and I have never, ever, ever forgotten that night. The family, even now, when we get together for Thanksgiving, we say, 'Remember that night Lily wore Cher's dress to the Oscars?!?'"

It would have been a touchstone for so many people, creating a bond between us that could never be broken. That's a real service to humanity. If we bumped into each other from time to time, on the street or at the movies, we wouldn't have to speak; no, we'd just look at each other, our heads bobbing up down with shared recall, our front teeth buried in our lower lips, a smile at the corners of our mouths. We might even feel so at one with each other that we'd make those whooping sounds that come with genuine ease and shared humor.

And it would someday be on my tombstone: *Remember that night she wore Cher's dress to the Oscars.*

But I didn't and none of it will ever be. I let everyone down, especially myself.

WHAT I LEARNED

Every day, take "your one wild and precious life" and fly.* The feather headdress would've helped. Just my luck.

*Paraphrasing Mary Oliver, "The Summer Day," 1992.

SHELDON SCHULTZ

President, TMG Artists Agency, Inc.

I dreamed about becoming the world's greatest, thinnest, handsomest operatic tenor! Nothing wrong with that notion. It was possible, and still is. All I had to do was study and practice, keep fit, maybe get a nose job and, if need be, a little Botox here and there. I looked around and saw a bunch of fat Italians and Swedes and felt there was a huge, unfilled opening in the marketplace for a guy who could sing like Pavarotti and looked like Paul Newman. Man, money would be the cheapest thing I got! Not to mention chicks. It's clear I never took the next important steps. Didn't follow the dream. Huge mistake! Not that I didn't have a wonderful career. My life has been very cool, and for the most part joyful, in spite of my mistake.

WHAT I LEARNED

In the final words of the great African drummer Baba Olatunji, "Live your life so when the time comes for the funeral the preacher won't have to bullshit the peoples."

JUDGE JUDY SHEINDLIN

Television Personality

If you're smart there are no mistakes—just learning experiences. Many years ago, when a woman attorney was about as welcome in the workplace as a skunk at a lawn party, I had one of those "learning experiences." My supervisor adopted one of my suggestions and passed it on as his own. I didn't confront him—I just boiled. It's one of those things that women often did, and still do, to ensure they were liked, as opposed to being respected and liked. Well, he was happy as a clam with all the accolades while I added two stress lines to my face.

WHAT I LEARNED

Trust me, it never happened again. In my professional world I strive to be respected—being liked is a bonus.

BARBARA FELDON

Actress (Agent 99, *Get Smart*)

One of the sharpest regrets I have can't be fixed. It involves the happiest year of my childhood and my sixth-grade teacher, Miss Pierce.

When I met her I was a chubby refugee from Hillcrest Grade School, a soot-encrusted stump of a building that squatted on a sea of gravel near a coal mining town south of Pittsburgh. While there I'd developed a florid school phobia. Every day I was tortured with anxiety inspired by our trucklike principal, who was also our fifth-grade writing teacher.

We could hear her in her office, pounding the bejesus out of some huge kid from Mine Three, the splat of her wooden paddle with a hole in middle, and her voice like Grendel's snarling, "I'm going to knock you through the wall!"

While we practiced the Peterson Method (round, round, ready, write, one, two, three . . .), dutifully curving *o*'s between blue lines on our pages, she would stalk massively up and down the aisles. When I felt her pause behind me I'd inwardly shrink; and then her huge fat hand would lower itself in front of my face, pounce on my page like a tarantula, crumple it, lift it a few pregnant inches, and drop it like a withered, contemptible ball before my stricken eyes.

That was the background to my entering, with shaking knees, Miss Pierce's sixth-grade class the following year when my family moved to a different school district in Pittsburgh.

Miss Pierce was angular, with severe hair and dark laser eyes—and she wasn't smiling. I soon realized she had no truck with being charming; she was only interested in *us*, seeing into each of us, gleaning the larval potential lurking there that she might bring to light.

She encouraged me to recite poetry (to this day my favorite way to perform), and her praise radiated through me like sunshine. She made algebra seem like magic and diagramming sentences like a game, and she enthralled us with stories about "thoroughbreds"—children who act honorably even in the worst of circumstances. Miss Pierce exposed us to the first classical music we'd ever heard; I remember eagerly listening for the horns growling in the Hall of the Mountain King in Edvard Grieg's Peer Gynt Suite.

Every day of that blessedly phobia-free year was an adventure, and I came away owning more of myself than I'd imagined existed.

One afternoon Miss Pierce told us a high school senior stopped her on the street to say how much her sixth-grade class had meant to him. She was touched he'd remembered her. Wondering how she could think any of us would ever forget her, I planned to return one day to prove I hadn't.

Years later, while in Pittsburgh doing promotion for *Get Smart,* I tried to find Miss Pierce, imagining she would still be in our beloved sixth-grade room. I was stunned to hear she had died several years earlier.

What I Learned

It was a painful but important lesson that it's perilous to put off thanking those who have touched one's life and heart. I'll forever regret postponing the gratitude that would have brought her pleasure. It can't be fixed—I can only offer it here. Thank you, Miss Pierce.

MARIO CUOMO

Governor of New York, 1983–1994

Ever since Adam nibbled at the forbidden fruit we have all been doomed to a life speckled with pimples where there might have been beauty marks, temptations we couldn't resist, and plain old mistakes in judgment. Some of the most regrettable of the mistakes are those made by politicians; they can wind up getting a nation into a war that wasn't necessary or an economy that's good for the few at the expense of the many, or they can mean even several years of wasted opportunity. I made a mistake like that in the campaign for president in 1988. I was reminded of it the other day by the candidate I supported and wanted desperately to win in that election, Governor Michael Dukakis.

There's no doubt in my mind that Mike, a three-term governor of Massachusetts who led his state to what was called the "Massachusetts Miracle," would have made a great president. He was, and still is, a man of superior intelligence, vast experience, unquestioned personal integrity, and a quiet and unassuming but unmistakable charm. By the end of the Democratic Convention most of the voters apparently agreed with that assessment. He was seventeen points ahead of George Herbert Walker Bush in the race, and there didn't seem to be any way Bush, who had a quiet and not well-known record as vice president, could catch him. But the Republicans had a secret weapon, a fiery, tough, and ruthless South Carolina political consultant named Lee Atwater who believed no blow was too low to be struck in a political fight. The Bush campaign went negative with an indecency and effectiveness that set a new and dismal standard for political mud wrestling. The best-remembered blow was the Willie Horton commercial that falsely suggested Mike had personally furloughed a convicted murderer who used the opportunity to rape a woman and kill her husband. Mike had nothing to do with the furlough; it wasn't even part of his governor's programs.

More attacks followed in a campaign later described as amazingly vicious, personal, and distorted. Phony smears were directed at Mike's wife, his loyalty to his religion, even his psychological health. Mike was obviously concerned about the attacks, especially those leveled at his lovely wife, and he turned to some of his advisers for suggestions. I was not a formal part of the campaign or even a major adviser, but he did ask me for an opinion as well. I had been through some difficult campaigns myself, and I'm sure he had that in mind.

My own attitude on campaigning was a lot like Mike's. It was summed up by a memorable line from an old Democratic congressional leader who said, "Any jackass can kick down a barn but it takes a good man to build one." Mike campaigned on the high road and didn't want to step down from it to start responding in kind to the Bush assault. The polls hadn't yet changed much, and so, with a degree of smugness, I told Mike he should ignore the attacks and continue going forward as he always had, making the case for himself and his policies proactively and criticizing Bush's views on the merits substantively. "You're no jackass, Mike!"

He stayed on the high road. Not long afterward the polls began to turn against him so swiftly that there was hardly time to reposition himself. In the end Mike lost, but the voters were obviously disgusted with the campaign; it was the lowest turnout since 1924.

I don't know how much of an influence my opinion had, but it was certainly not helpful. In fact it was, as Mike and I later agreed, some of the worst advice I had ever given.

WHAT I LEARNED

What I should have added to the old Democratic congressional leader's good line was "But when the jackass starts kicking down the barn, a good man should start kicking the jackass!"

NANCY COYNE

CEO, Serino Coyne Advertising Agency

A pilot was flying from Los Angeles to Hawaii, and a visitor sitting in the cockpit—this was back in the "good old days"—was listening in on the communication from the tower.

"Correct five degrees southwest."

A few minutes later: "Correct ten degrees northwest."

And then, "Correct ten degrees southeast."

"Aren't you ever *on course?*" the visitor asked the pilot.

"'On course' is just like life: a series of corrections," the pilot replied.

In hindsight, it's hard to call anything a mistake inasmuch as the lessons learned from mistakes make them seem like necessary steps on the path to success. But certainly if I were to use my life as a road map to advise my daughter where the potholes were, I'd look at the decision I made to get married at twenty-one. I was still in college, and immediate gratification wasn't fast enough. "Carpe diem" beat the hell out of "Good things come to those who wait."

As the marriage progressed—it lasted over twenty years—it became clear that certain fundamental differences between us would be our undoing. He was Catholic. I wasn't much of anything. He was one of seven. I was an only child. He liked to hunt. The sight of a gun makes me crazy with loathing. He grew up in a town in South Dakota with plenty of bars and no bookstore. I grew up outside Washington, D.C., and did my homework in the Library of

Congress. I am ambitious. He likes a good nap. As my career progressed, his stalled, and instead of trying harder, he expressed real satisfaction with the status quo.

So when I finally left him, my decision cost me quite a lot. He got both homes and the contents, both cars, and all his guns, and I had to write a big check to boot. The case never went to a judge. I chose to give all that, as he could have asked for half of my business based on the longevity of the marriage.

When the cashed check came back from the bank, for some reason I carried it around with me. I'd take it out and look at it in taxis or while waiting for a client to show up at lunch. I'd actually had to borrow the money to pay him off in one fell swoop, so at forty-five I was starting over, with debt, but also with a career that was flourishing. I often said that if my husband had told a judge, "I made her what she is today," he wouldn't have been lying. Having to pay all the bills for our life in New York, our nanny/housekeeper, our daughter's private school, and our weekend place in Connecticut had been an incredible incentive. And make no mistake, my ex was not a househusband with dinner waiting when I got home.

Soon, when the canceled check began to feel like something other than evidence of my early bad choices, it began to simply represent the price I paid for my freedom. It started to feel like proof of my value. After all, as my therapist asked, "Would you rather be the one who had to ask for a check or the one who could write it?" I came to love that canceled check. Because of my "mistake," not a day goes by that I don't feel like a million bucks.

WHAT I LEARNED

Character is a lot more important than chemistry. Character is much more likely to endure.

MARTIN SHEEN

Award-Winning Actor

In the spring of 1988, I went to the United Farm Workers headquarters in Delano, California, with my son Emilio to support César Chávez in his fast for life. Although I had never met him, Chávez had been a great source of personal inspiration for me since he had cofounded the UFW union with Dolores Huerta in 1962.

Hailed as one of the greatest Mexican American civil rights leaders, whose work led to numerous improvements for migrant farmworkers, Chávez had been inspired by the nonviolent examples of Mahatma Gandhi and Martin Luther King Jr. By organizing the workers and confronting the growers with boycotts, strikes, nonviolent protest, and long personal fasts, he achieved a level of justice with a measure of dignity for farmworkers unimaginable in the history of American agriculture.

Now he had chosen to fast once again at great personal risk in order to draw public awareness to the indiscriminate use of deadly pesticides dumped on field crops with the residual effects of illness and sometimes even cancer among the field workers and their families.

Events at Delano began in the afternoon with a news conference to identify the deadly pesticides at issue and announce the start of the "fast for life," which aimed to help bring about an end to their use. In the evening a mass was celebrated at a makeshift altar in the union hall, followed by a rally attended by supporters and thousands of rank and file. This routine of mass and rally would last throughout the fast and in the weeks that followed. I returned every few days to participate in both. The mass was the only public event Chávez attended during the fast. Every evening, accompanied by his wife, Helen, and followed by other family members, friends, and union officials in a solemn procession, he walked from a small workers' bungalow a few hundred yards to the hall. His arrival was greatly anticipated by a huge crowd inside the hall, who stood to greet him in profound silence as he made his entrance.

On the afternoon of the twenty-third day of the fast for life, I arrived at Delano with my wife, Janet, and two old friends, Father Bill O'Donnell, who was also a close friend of Chávez's, and Dr. Davida Coady. As we waited for the evening mass, Father Bill casually asked if we would like to meet Chávez. I was excited at the possibility, of course, but I had been given to believe that he was not receiving visitors during the fast. Father Bill thought an exception might be made if we were interested. Naturally, I said we'd be honored. With that, Father Bill went off to make the arrangements and returned in half an hour to announce that Chávez was waiting to receive us! I could barely contain my joy, but the anticipation of meeting my hero was overwhelming, and during the walk from the hall to the bungalow I lit a cigarette to calm my nerves. I had been a heavy smoker all of my adult life, and a cigarette had become a natural remedy for any stress. As we arrived at the bungalow, Father Bill and Davida went in straightaway, but I lingered to finish my cigarette. "Put that out and come inside," Janet commanded. "You go ahead, I'll be right in," I responded. Exasperated, she left me standing outside as I took a deep final puff, then flipped the cigarette away and went inside.

The room was small and the light was low, but I could see Janet bending beside a single bed, where Chávez lay. He seemed much smaller than I had imagined as Janet kissed his hand and he kissed hers. Then I was called forward by Father Bill, who introduced me as Ramon Estevez, which is my real name. I knelt down in reverence to kiss his hand. He held on to mine and returned the gesture, kissing the very spot where I had just held the cigarette. I was humiliated, embarrassed, and deeply ashamed, because I knew for Chávez it was like kissing an ashtray, and in that instant I made a vow in the secret depths of my heart that I would stop smoking for as long as he fasted.

Over the next two weeks, César's health declined rapidly as he approached a point of no return. But as he grew weaker, public support for his cause grew stronger, culminating with the arrival at Delano of the Reverend Jesse Jackson, who proposed a form of compromise to help end the fast. His plan was inspired. César could end his fast if enough of his supporters would be willing to take it up by fasting three days each, then passing it on from one to another, thus making the fast indefinite. Also, the person who was fasting would wear one of the little crosses made from grapevines around his or her neck as a sign of solidarity and commitment.

This proposal was greeted with overwhelming support and enthusiasm at the mass that evening, and the following day César ended the fast after thirty-six days. I joined the three-day fast and began my nonsmoking vow simultaneously, but when I reached the thirty-sixth day of not smoking, I decided to continue on in homage to César Chávez and I did not smoke again for fourteen years.

What I Learned

Sometimes our needs feel overwhelming, but a focus on the bigger picture can keep us from indulging in them.

PETER FALK

Actor

When I was three years old my preschool teacher called my mother and said she wondered if there was something wrong with my eyes. Many times during the day I would cock my head in this unnatural way in order to look at something. She wondered right. The doctor told my mother I had cancer of the eye and it had to be removed and yesterday was not too soon.

My mother, God love her, moved fast. She took me to two more doctors that same day, and they all said the same thing: it was a cancerous tumor—a well-known eye cancer, retina blastoma—and it could kill. I was operated on two days later. Probably the earliest memory of my life was being in the hospital on the morning of the operation, standing in front of the elevator with my mother. When the elevator arrived my mother said, "Oh my goodness, I forgot my pocketbook," and then she told me to get in the elevator and tell the doctor to wait, she'd be right back. I was three, and I remember getting out of the elevator where there were men all in white. I told them to wait for my mother, she was getting her pocketbook. That was the last thing I remember about that day.

The next earliest memory was running around a large room eating an apple and talking to a lot of adults who were lying in beds but not saying anything. I also remember standing in front of a store window, my mother's hand on my shoulder, looking at photographs of men wearing black eye patches and my mother asking me which

I liked best. Obviously the experience made a deep impression on me. Eventually I was fitted for a glass eye.

As I was growing up, I recall dreading the moment when some kid would ask, "Hey, what's the matter with your eye? It looks funny" or "How come one eye moves and the other don't?" This sensitivity started decreasing in my early teens and was completely gone by high school. The kids were always electing me president. I felt comfortable with everybody and played sports. I hung out with the guys on the street corner and in poolrooms where everybody needled anybody about anything—it was a very healthy atmosphere for me. That's where I learned I could get a laugh.

At Ossining High School the baseball field was right in back of the school and the grandstand was very close to the playing field, particularly on the third base side. This is significant because on this particular day it was a play at third base and the umpire called me out. It was a bad call. I was clearly safe. I knew it and everybody in the stands knew it. They sat so close to the field, they could see and hear everything. In front of everyone, I whipped out my eye and handed it to the umpire: "You'll do better with this one." Talk about getting a laugh. I got a roar. Even the guys on the other team were rolling in the grass.

I once went in for an eye test—you know, the one where you read the letters of the alphabet on a chart that's hanging on the wall. The guy conducting the test looked like he'd been doing this for a lot of years. To put it mildly, he was not too interested. He mumbled hello, indicated a chair. I sat down and he said, "We'll start with the left eye." So I covered the right eye and read the chart with my left, and he wrote down the numbers. He then said, "Now we'll do the right eye." I said, "The right eye is glass." He said, "Well, do the best you can."

The early eyes were all glass. The plastic ones didn't come in until the late 1960s. When I was a kid, the doctors told me to make sure that every night I took out the glass eye and put it into a glass of water. Naturally, after doing this for sixteen years, you get sloppy—you forget, there's not a glass handy, you're drunk, you're tired, whatever. I would frequently just toss the eye under the pillow.

I was attracted to a young lady who had a Pekingese that sometimes slept with her. One night she afforded me the same privilege as the Pekingese. The following morning, I looked under the pillow—no eye. You guessed it! There was the Pekingese—a pig in shit—crunching away on my eye. Until they brought in plastic, that's the last time I slept in a bed that included a Pekingese.

Over the years, I went to four colleges—one of them was Hamilton. There, I got lucky. The four guys living across the dorm hall were extraordinarily funny, vital guys who introduced me to the world of ideas. For this story you need only know one of these guys—Pete Woitoch. A boy wonder physicist on a science scholarship, Pete played fabulous jazz piano. Art Tatum at that time—and even now, fifty years later—was arguably the planet's number one jazz pianist. Tatum passed through Utica, New York, regularly to play a local nightclub. Whenever he was there, he called Woitoch and invited him to sit in. I didn't know this. So the three guys came into my room and told me about Tatum and the invitation for that night and how we were all going. I should have been thrilled, but I wasn't.

When I had woken up that morning I couldn't find my eye. I remembered putting it down on an end table, but when I looked it wasn't there. I explained this to the guys, and when I said I couldn't go, they wouldn't hear of it. "It's a nightclub—it's dark—nobody is looking at you. They're interested in Tatum, in themselves, in Woitoch—not in you." Actually, what they were saying made sense—I knew I could keep my lid closed and I was dying to go, so I relented. We headed out to the club.

What a great evening. The crowd loved Pete—so did Tatum—and when it got late and the place emptied, the five of us stood around the piano listening to Tatum play. Art liked his gin and usually had a jigger within reach. At one point, playing with only one hand, he slid the jigger in my direction. "I've had enough," he said. "Help yourself—it's world-class gin."

I liked the idea of drinking Art Tatum's gin, so I lifted the jigger not to make a toast but as a gesture of gratitude in his direction. Then I noticed something at the bottom of the jigger; my glass eye—sitting there in the gin, at the bottom of that jigger. MY GLASS EYE!

Those sons of bitches—my buddies from across the hall—they had stolen my eye and set me up. I can still see Tatum laughing—his shoulders shaking, the tears running down his cheeks, his hand reaching for a handkerchief, wiping the water from his eyes. It was a beautifully crafted scam. I'll give 'em that.

WHAT I LEARNED

My mistake was in not realizing that a glass eye doesn't just disappear from an end table. I should have been onto them. I also learned that there can be humor in things you'd never imagine, especially if you've had a few drinks.

JOHN HOPE BRYANT

Founder, Chairman, and CEO, Operation HOPE

M y life makes sense to me.

What I mean by this is that everything I do today is personal to me and reflects lessons learned from and through the education of living a full life: all instructed in some way by the way I grew up in South Central Los Angeles and Compton, California.

I remember my mother, Ms. Juanita Smith, telling me she loved me every day, and as a result I never really had much of a self-esteem problem as a child. My father, Mr. Johnnie Will Smith, made a payroll out of the front door of our home as the owner of Johnnie Cement Works, which gave me a powerful sense of "yes, I can." I am sure that led me to starting my first business, the Neighborhood Candy House, at age ten. I borrowed $40 from my mother, who just wanted me to stop bugging her and "go away," and made $300 a week—at ten years old. But then I found girls and lost the business. This was a recurring theme in my life for a while. Later, friends would always ask me the same question: "How did you get it in your mind that you could start a business at age ten?" My response? "It never dawned on me that I couldn't. You see, I saw my father do it."

From my mother I got a powerful sense of self-esteem and self-love. That is why I often say there is a difference between being broke and being poor. Being broke is a temporary economic condition, but being poor is a disabling state of mind and a depressed condition of your spirit—you must vow to never, ever be poor again.

Seeing my father pay his employees every week from the front door of our home gave me a powerful sense of purpose. He was literally giving these men life and the dignity of providing for their families. But I also learned from my dad the power of financial literacy, or financial illiteracy. You see, my dad has owned his own business for more than fifty years now and did a fine job raising me and my brother and sister, but my dad was not financially literate. As a result, my brilliant father would often make $1 but manage to spend $1.50 and, worse still, not know it. He would meet the local community mortgage broker with a smile, and trust, asking only the loan payment amount but never the interest rate. You can finance a $400 iPod and end up years later having paid a whopping $5,000 for it over time. Just imagine the interest rate on a thirty-year mortgage.

Financial disagreements are the number one reason for divorce in America today, and money was at the heart of my loving parents' ultimate divorce when I was a child. Today, my mom lives financially independent in Houston, Texas, and my brilliant father lives with me, or shall I say in a new three-unit apartment building I built for him. This is why I am passionate about financial literacy and why Operation HOPE has educated more than two hundred thousand low-wealth youths in financial literacy to date. Because it is not about making more money, but making better decisions with the money you make.

Probably the greatest lesson I learned from what I call Life University was when I was eighteen years old. You see, after years of believing too much of my own press as a very mediocre actor, and making countless bad decisions based on my ego and not good business sense or common sense, I went from living in a rented beach house in Malibu, California, to living in my Jeep behind a florist near the Los Angeles airport. That's right, I was homeless for six months of my life when I was eighteen. Worse still, the world I knew had written me off because, frankly, I was not a very nice person and many thought I got what I deserved. Well, it took me years to understand that that entire false ego I was carrying around was nothing more than insecurity and low self-esteem revisited. Obviously, I had not listened to my mother long enough. But when my mother could not get through to me, God found a way to communicate. Someone once told me, "Sometimes God has to tear you down in order to be able to build you back up." This was certainly the case in my life.

I rebuilt my life, because sitting there alone in the back of that leased Montero Jeep, I realized that I may have made a mistake, but *I* was not a mistake. I was God's child, and He had a plan and destiny that was all mine. It had my name on it, alone. All I had to do was claim it. And I had to get out of my own way too. One of my mentors is Ambassador Saburo Yuzawa of Japan. I remember on one of my trips to visit him he told me, "John, the whole purpose of life is to be transparent to God's will." I said, "Wow, how do I do that?" His response: "Learn to get out of your own way." Enough said.

At the end of the day, I could not blame the white man for my being homeless. I could not blame the Ku Klux Klan for my being homeless. I could not blame my mother or my father for my being homeless. I could only blame me. I was the maker of my destiny, and I had screwed this one up but good. But once again, "God doesn't make dirt," and I knew that my hopes and dreams were just as valuable as anyone else's. I simply had to assume responsibility for achieving them. I guess that is why I am such a personal responsibility junkie today. My life taught me that, quoting author Deepak Chopra, "the universe has a perfect accounting system." Whatever goes around comes around. That's good news if you are putting good news out every day into the world, and trying your best to serve others and humanity, while at the same time advancing your own unique goals, dreams, and desires.

WHAT I LEARNED

I also learned something spectacularly important: that you cannot have a rainbow without a storm first. That your problems are actually essential for your growth in this life. That without problems, without legitimate suffering, you don't grow. That education and knowledge come from books and schools, but wisdom comes from God and experience. We need both.

What I learned was to embrace my potential and my pain in life.

I learned to redefine success as "going from failure to failure without loss of enthusiasm."

I learned that I should not let compliments go to my head, nor criticisms to my heart.

I learned that God doesn't make dirt, and even when you make a mistake, you are not a mistake.

I learned that a saint is a sinner that got up.

I learned that you cannot have a rainbow without a storm first.

NANCY A. GRACE

CNN Headline News Anchor

I prosecuted felony cases for nearly a decade in one of the oldest, grandest courthouses in the South, the Atlanta Fulton County Courthouse. The courtrooms were vast and marble-floored, with high wooden benches for the judges, huge long oak tables for counsel, and rows and rows of wooden pews for spectators and witnesses. The district attorney was housed in the same courthouse. Sitting there at my desk in the late afternoon, working up a trial, I heard the calendar clerk coming down the hall pushing a cart containing a huge load of cases. She plopped a big stack of brand-new manila folders onto my desk. Each had a label across the top with a defendant's name and a number—an indictment number. I started sorting through.

Reading each folder, I skimmed through the usual car thefts, burglaries, shopliftings, drug possession and trafficking—the whole criminal code was represented. I pulled out two new murder cases and one aggravated child molestation case as the most serious and most time-consuming to prepare for trial. That was the first moment I learned the name Walter Gates, charged with aggravated child molestation. I read the entire file and knew instinctively I was in for a fight, and the defendant, Walter Gates, had plenty of money to fight back: he was a millionaire. He had cornered the Atlanta market on the tourist trade of horse-drawn carriage rides through parks, historical sites, and downtown Atlanta. He branched out from there into limo services and the transportation trade in general. He had also hired some of the best criminal defense attorneys in the business.

What also caught my eye were the ages of the victims, just five and seven years old. My stomach clenched when I saw the addresses of the victims and the molester: they were the same. I called my investigator, Ernest, and we walked out of the courthouse within the hour to go to the house.

The home was lovely, much nicer than the place I rented near the courthouse. We did a slow drive-by and checked out the neighborhood, the cars in the driveway, whatever we could see. It was straight out of *Leave It to Beaver*. My first question was why the victims and the alleged molester lived in the same home. I quickly deduced that the girls' mother turned a blind eye to what was happening and allowed her children's molester to live in her home. This affirmed a phenomenon I've yet to understand: women siding with husbands, boyfriends, live-ins, or exes over their own children, choosing to ignore the monster under their roof. In this case, the live-in, Walter Gates, was also the mother's employer, for whom she had worked for a very long time.

We rang the doorbell—no answer. Ernest knocked on the door frame loudly with the butt of his police walkie-talkie. We waited, convinced someone was home, but no one ever answered. As we drove away, I looked back, feeling someone was there who couldn't or wouldn't come to the door. I did the only thing I could at that point: investigate through research.

After a few days of digging, including going to the district attorney archives building to find files more than twenty years old, I discovered there were child molestation allegations against Walter Gates going back decades, and to date, he had served not one day of hard jail time. I remember finding a twenty-year-old original police report on yellowed paper, typed with a manual police station typewriter. It was from a "school detective" who wrote a narrative of

Gates's natural daughter, twelve years old at the time, coming to school with a horrible black eye, her lips swollen and bloody. She told school detectives outright that her father had raped her, beating her viciously when she resisted. The case was never pursued. Nothing happened. Someone chose to do nothing.

All the other cases also dealt with numerous children, stepchildren, and little daughters of Gates's girlfriends. Why? Either money or influence must have kept him insulated from the justice system, and I was determined these would be the last children he touched.

The morning I finally got to meet the two little sisters in the case in chief, my heart broke. They were beautiful, shy, quiet, and smart. Their starched dresses were lovely and detailed, their hair adorned with multiple little colored barrettes. On the outside, they were perfect, untouched, like two porcelain dolls. I looked at the mom and couldn't help but question her harshly. She claimed she didn't believe her own daughters and that her husband, Walter Gates, would never touch them in that way. But their medical exams said differently: neither girl had a hymen left, indicating not just fondling but full-blown sexual intercourse. When I explained this to the mother, she seemed not to hear me. I kept saying it until she blurted out defensively that somebody else must have done it . . . not him.

I took the girls together away from the mom and spoke to them. They were clearly afraid, but once away from their mom, and with slow, measured baby steps, they explained to me exactly who had been molesting them and how. They spoke in the language of children, a language adults don't always understand. It is a language that has to be unlocked to interpret. Sometimes little children can't identify dates or exact times, so I rely on timing by events like the Christmas tree being up or a birthday party. Instead of street addresses, locations like "near the grocery" or "behind the school" suffice to establish jurisdiction. Once the code was cracked, the sisters' message was clear. They absolutely had been molested by their mother's live-in.

I began to investigate the "similar transactions," other little girls

Gates was accused of molesting, accused but never prosecuted. I found one of the oldest daughters I mentioned earlier, now all grown up but seemingly defeated by life. We sat together in her one room, on the bed, and she described her father, Gates, molesting her for the first time. She was the one who resisted and was beaten black and blue. She was twelve. She went to school the next day with a black eye, swollen and battered. She told her teacher. She told the school detective. Nothing happened, except she went home each day after school and the abuse continued.

I found another victim. She was gorgeous and articulate. She hadn't grown up with her biological father, Walter Gates, but instead lived with her mom in another state. On her first visit to her biological father for the summer at age fourteen, he took her out to the stables where he housed all the livery horses and raped her. In stark contrast to the destroyed lives of her half sisters, she had gone on to write a book on the subject and lecture across the country. I then found the teenage sister of the two current victims. She had moved out of the beautiful home they had and into some of the worst housing projects in the city of Atlanta in order to get away. He had been assaulting children for years.

Enter the lawyers. One, a noted defense attorney (and part-time judge!), was defending Gates. It would become one of the most wrenching trials I ever worked. The weekend before the trial, while I honed the witness list and wrote my opening statement and direct examinations of each witness, the defense got busy too, but with a very different strategy. They had the mother of these two little girls bring them to the defense attorney's offices over the weekend.

I found out that the little girls had apparently recanted only when the lead attorney announced it in his opening statement before the jury. I nearly blew a gasket. How could they do such a thing? My objections became more and more angry and confrontational, thereby making the judge more and more angry at me. Remember, the defense lawyer was his brethren, a fellow judge, albeit part-time!

In a final move to drive the recantation home to the jury in a way no five-year-old ever could, the defense lawyer put his own law partner on the stand, who "happened" to be there at the law offices that Saturday to witness the so-called recantations of the little girls. I crossed him with a vengeance, and it was hard to do. The law partner was one of those guys that just ooze charm—smooth-talking, calm, and cool. After a series of questions that were getting me nowhere, I hit upon a line of questioning: money. This was all about money. The mom was suported by Gates, the family lived off him, the lead attorney was making thousands off the defense, and the law partner–witness would share in the fees. It was sick. I would cross him on his pecuniary, or monetary, interest in the outcome of the case.

The minute I got the question out regarding Gates's huge retainer, counsel roared an objection, claiming any and all fees were secret, subject to the attorney-client privilege. The trial judge overruled me in front of the jury and gave a lecture from the bench on attorney-client privilege and the sanctity of a lawyer's confidential business dealings, ending with the observation that I didn't know the law. I believed I did.

Firmly recalling my memory of the OCGA (Official Code of Georgia Annotated), I turned directly to the witness and did it again. I asked the very same question just overruled.

The judge, furious, red-faced, and yelling, sent out the jury and admonished me. He also promised to hold me in contempt, which could require at least one night in jail and a stiff fine. I could also get in trouble with the Georgia Bar Association. I stood there wondering if I could lose that thing dearest to me, my license to practice law.

I agreed to refrain from doing it again, and sat down in my seat. I was so mortified, I couldn't even look up from my lap, much less into the eyes of a triumphant defendant and defense lawyer. My face was hot. I accepted the judge's ruling. I would keep my law license and stay out of jail. As a government worker, I didn't have money for a big fine, anyway. When the jury came back in, I would announce "nothing further" and cease questioning. I waited and the jury began to file back into the box. It was time to eat a dirt sandwich and back down.

I glanced up and caught one of the jurors returning a smile to the defense partner still sitting on the witness stand as the jury walked back in. It made me sick inside. The jury believed there was no money connection, that the line of cross-exam was wrong. They would never understand that this was all about money and not at all about the truth. At least the two little girls were no longer in the courtroom and I didn't have to meet their eyes.

The judge turned to me. "Ms. Grace?"

My mouth was dry and I could hear blood pounding in my ears. Backing down to avoid jail on contempt had been a horrible mistake. My mistake in accepting the judge's ruling was grievous. The children's recantation would be accepted and Gates would walk free. The mistake was bigger than me, bigger than the courtroom. I stood.

"Isn't it true this is ALL ABOUT MONEY? You and your partner will make a mint off this case . . . Those little girls didn't truly recant!" Words to that effect hung in the air for a split second.

Then, all hell broke lose. Books fell, papers flew, the judge banged the gavel, leaping up off his leather swivel chair, and he ordered the jury out. He immediately held me in contempt, and before you could blink your eyes, the courtroom filled with troops and troops from the public defender's office, thrilled to have a front-row seat to see me cuffed and hauled off to jail.

It was all worth it. The jury got it. They convicted. The night of the guilty verdict, I got long-distance calls from four locations across the country, all from women who had been molested by Walter Gates. Their cases had never been prosecuted. We toasted long-distance . . . to Lady Justice and her sword.

WHAT I LEARNED

I learned in one blinding moment, in the face of an enormous mistake: Believe in what you know to be true and *be ready to fight for it*. Be cold or hot, but never lukewarm. And last, if it's worth having, it's worth fighting for. And you can sometimes prevent a bad mistake right in the middle of making it.

P.S. I didn't end up in jail, and even better, the appeals court agreed with me. I did know the law after all . . . at least that time!

ROSIE O'DONNELL

Comedian, Actress, Advocate

My father filled out my college applications. A lot of people tell me this is weird. Not to me. Left to my own devices, or lack thereof, I would never have gone.

College was important in my family. There was no "if" we were going, only where. My father sacrificed to make sure we all had access to the best universities. Why? I don't know. I figure he thought it would ensure our financial futures. It was the way he made it out of where he was to where he is now—a far better place. My father grew up in the tenements. He had a secret, mysterious childhood that was, I'm sure, as much responsible for his deficits as his strengths. I tried when I was a teenager to get him to talk about what had happened to him. Had he himself been hurt? Neglected? Abused? He always avoided these conversations. He'd say, "That doesn't matter. What matters, Dolly, is you getting a good education." College. I didn't want to go. I wanted to be a comedienne.

My father sent away for the brochures, all those shrink-wrapped booklets showing blond students on brick walls. It's not that I wasn't tempted to enter such a world. I just knew, right from the start, that it wasn't gonna fit me. It didn't.

Dickinson College, in Carlisle, Pennsylvania, accepted "me." It was a good school, full of a bunch of kids a lot smarter than I was. The campus was too cute. There were elm trees and little gardens. There was a playing field chalked with neat white lines, as though space, the world, can be fairly divided. Leading up to the dorms there were pathways lined with trees that bore berries that looked delicious but were poisonous. I was sure that murderers loomed in those trees, waiting to assault a wandering coed. I would never go out at night alone.

There was a pub on campus called the Hub. Which sounds quite Dr. Seuss–esque. I hung out there a lot. Too much. I would imagine myself with Dave Mangus, the junior boy who looked so much like this new actor Tom Cruise who had just starred in *Risky Business*. He was, my Tommy, from the moment I saw him, the most handsome man I'd ever seen. Remains true today, twenty some odd years later. His double, Dave Mangus, kissed me once there in the Hub pub.

I first spoke to Chrissie in Professor Betty Barnes's environmental science class. I had seen her the day before in anthropology. She had red sweatpants and a white sweatshirt—no zipper—with a hood. It had that worn-out, preppy, no-flea-market look to it. She had a blond ponytail, two notebooks, and a Snyder's hard pretzel in her hand. She was beautiful in a non-magazine way. She looked like she'd walked out of a J. Crew catalog.

I saw her and I knew immediately I would love her, and there was nothing sexual about it. Not then. A full five months later, though, I would be throwing up every time she was near me. Then, I would say, it became sexual in my mind, or at least the option of it did. I puked. Go figure. I would puke almost every morning; the other girls on my hall were convinced I was pregnant. No, just gay. And, for the first time, sexually awake.

One evening, I came home from a study hall and the dorm was strangely quiet. It was early, but for some reason the lights in most of the windows were off, and the entryway was dark. Just a few weeks back there'd been some crime on campus, a petty burglary, a brandished knife, and a warning had gone out. I stood in the hallway then, my back pressed to the wall. Something didn't feel right, but when I looked around me, nothing exactly was wrong. The moonlight flowed in through the common room window, landing on the TV with its bent rabbit ears, the floor littered with wrappers and bright blobs of gum. "Hello?" I called out, stupidly, as though this were a home and not a sixty-person dorm, and no one answered me. Silence.

I climbed the echoing steps and came out on floor two, where the hall light was on, bright and violent. I blinked. There was still silence. I looked for signs of the struggle, blood-soaked clothes. Nothing. I went upstairs to the TV room, and there sat sixty silent women, crying, glued to the TV set. John Lennon had been killed in New York City. John Lennon was dead. Chrissie was bereft. I wanted to touch her.

I didn't know, exactly, that I was gay. I did know that sex terrified me; ever since the seventh grade, when the boy-midget of my class had kissed me, I'd felt terror at the prospect of touch. I did know that when I'd gone out with kids in high school, where I'd been popular, I was always the designated driver, waiting with the car keys while they did it with each other on the beach, and I stood separate, and safe. I'd had the occasional thought, for some reason always in a car when I was driving, that perhaps I was a lesbian, and in my giddier moments I'd even shouted it out, just to hear it, but the words never moved me much, and I forgot about them as soon as I said them. Being a lesbian didn't interest me much back then. I wasn't worried about being gay or straight. I was mostly worried about avoiding sex with anyone, anywhere, anytime.

I did not sleep well in college. What with the murdered Beatle, Three Mile Island, mass murderers, and Chrissie three flights up.

I don't really remember what we talked about the first time we had lunch together, just that we talked, that words were easy between us. I remember what she ate, a salad from the salad bar with bright yellow shredded cheese on top, and cherry tomatoes as cheery as holiday ornaments. I remember watching her lift a cherry tomato with her fork, how first she pierced it so a spurt of seeds came out the sides, and then she raised it to her tongue, and then she chewed, the fruit's juice making her lips go glossy. I was mesmerized. She was everything I wasn't, but for some reason that didn't make me feel bad, as it had with the other college girls. She showed me all her stuff. I loved her stuff. She loved my humor. She let everyone on campus know that I was a seriously funny person, and my stock rose.

After classes we'd go back to her room and rifle her closet. I tried on her shirts and skirts. I told her about my past—not everything, but a lot. I told her about the broken-down house on Rhonda Lane, the cancer and my mother. She told me her mother was Norwegian, her dad a professor at Temple University. That impressed me. She got excellent grades and I never saw her study. I sometimes studied, and my grades sucked. Sometimes, trying on her clothes, I'd ask her to button me up the back. Then I could feel her fingers on my spine and it made me, quite simply, want to cry. After one of these instances, I'd go back to my own dorm room, exhausted by the intensity of my feelings, fall onto my bed, and sink into a deep sleep.

Then Chrissie and I started staying up all night, talking. I started to count the hours till I would see her again, and to experience the hours away from her as just filler. We drank beer at the pub and studied science together and somehow it happened, that after a late night of talking, or trying on clothes, somehow it wound up that we started sleeping together in the same bed. There was nothing sexual going on, yet the word got out—we were lezzies. Her mother, who was very cool and beautiful, said, "Are you and Chrissie lovers?" We both said no, and she said, "So why are you so worried?"

But the talk increased. One night I gave Chris a back rub. I could feel the tension in her muscles; I could feel her flinch when I touched her. We had the light on, a lamp on the bedside table, its shade chenille—soft, small dots. I worked her shoulders, her spine, and then the small of her back, where we hold our hurts. I would not have gone any lower, had no plans to go any lower. I placed my palms flat on the small of her back and pushed in. I pushed the pads of my fingertips into her thin skin and watched, when I lifted them, the fading ovals on her back.

"Chrissie," I said, in a voice all raw.

"Okay," she said, her own voice muffled in the pillow, and then she lifted her head. "Okay, Roseann, enough." And then she shook me off and walked across the room, and we stood there, staring at each other.

After that, things changed between us. I started throwing up again. She stopped eating. Sometime around the middle of November, she came to me. "People are saying we're gay," she said. "We can't hang out in my room alone."

"Who cares what they're saying," I said. I paused. My voice rose. "And so what if we're gay?"

Chrissie looked at me. She looked at me long and hard. "I'm not gay," she said, and for the first time I noticed a twitch in her eyes. She was afraid.

The snow started early that year, pre-Thanksgiving. It fell in dry white flakes, as light as package stuffing. That was when I saw a starving squirrel on my window ledge, its tail a piece of gimpy cartilage, its fur battered. And then it died. That night, it was cold, so cold that shovels shattered on the sidewalk when you tried to use them, and the moon was frosted over. Back at home, I stood with my sister in the bathroom, and I told her I was in love and not sure what to do about it. For some people, making this claim is shattering and revelatory, but for me it was a clear confirmation of what I had always known. It was not revealing but confirming.

When I returned after the new year, Chrissie was sick. She'd grown, with no warning, terribly thin. You could see the planking of bone on her face. You could see the strings stretched taut in her neck. You could see the fanning of ribs, like the piping of bird bone in a wing. "Chrissie," I said, coming up to her in the cafeteria, where she was fretting over the iceberg lettuce at the salad bar. "Chrissie, what happened?"

She refused to discuss it. I was wrong. Nothing had happened. She had no idea what I was talking about. And so we finally drifted apart. No more sleepovers. No more nights of quarters and beers.

Her life revolved around the food in the cafeteria, the stuff she would not taste. She had the menu memorized but she would eat only salad, with the occasional Bac-Os.

The year ended. I packed up my rented car, told the girls on my floor I'd be right back. I was just going to get some chips for our goodbye party. I watched Chris watch me drive away. She knew I wasn't coming back. I didn't. I've never been good at goodbyes.

As for Chris, she ended up going back to Norway, where she worked out her food issues. She married a man she loves and has two babies. Sometimes now, when I am walking down the street and I see a woman with a long blond braid, I think it's Chrissie, still, after all these years, and I experience it all over again, the saltwater-spray-in-the-lungs feeling of first love. Then it goes. The person passes me by.

Six years ago, after fifteen years of not having spoken a word to her, I got a letter out of the Nordic blue from Chrissie. That's when she told me about her husband and kids. She also told me in that letter that she finally wanted to talk about our freshman year in college. But there was nothing left to say. At last, at last, I told her I'd loved her purely. I told her that she'd changed my life by loving me back, and—no matter what—it would stay that way. It was what it was.

As I write this now, I wonder where in this story lies my big mistake, the biggest one I ever made. Why did Chrissie come to mind when thinking about my most serious failure? If I were to ask my teachers from that single college year (I never graduated), they would say the mistake in this story happened when I drove away at the end, and for good. But if I were to ask myself—and I am now asking myself—where the single most serious mistake here lies, I might say it was simply, and irrevocably, in the passage of time: how long it took me to tell her that I loved her. It took more than twenty years.

What I Learned

I am forty-four now. I awake some nights soaked in sweat: the menacing midlife change. Time moves swiftly, pages torn from a book. As a woman I have learned what I did not know as a girl: that the stellar detritus that makes us up is but the briefest form; in the blink of an eye it's gone, and you lose your classification, whatever it may be—gay, woman, mother, daughter, friend. In the blink of an eye, we lose our humanity, slip back into space, and become a part of the galaxy—planets, stars, holes—from which we once came. I took what seems a long time to say I was gay, but longer still to learn to say "I love you."

Someone did a study on the cell phone calls made from the Twin Towers as they fell. The question: Was there any pattern in what people said? The researchers expected they would find repeated SOSes—pleas for life, asking for absolution—but there was remarkably little of that. Instead, what the people said over and over again as they died, what they sent out across the sea of static: "I love you." These words, when said sincerely, have the capacity to right our wrongs, and live on long after we have gone back to being stars.

NICHOLAS PERRICONE, MD

World-Renowned Antiaging Expert, Bestselling Author

As the late afternoon's twilight faded into night, a fierce wind-driven sleet rattled the windows and shrieked in the chimneys. I hurried through the drafty corridors and breezeways of the hospital, feeling the February chill seeping into my tired bones. Twenty-nine hours and counting, I said to myself, over and over, not knowing when this interminable shift would end. I struggled against the exhaustion that threatened to overtake me and put a premature end to my unfinished rounds. Both my mood and my future appeared bleak—long days, longer nights, sleep deprivation, high stress, crushing fatigue, and the constant pressure and responsibility of caring for seriously ill children in endless succession.

Such was life during my internship in pediatrics at the Yale University School of Medicine. It was not much different from that of any other intern; however, this night would turn out to be one I would never forget.

I headed toward the admissions desk in anticipation of greeting one of my favorite patients, a bright and cheerful nine-year-old slated for cardiac surgery in the morning.

Carrie's smiling face and calm demeanor belied the harrowing experience she was about to undergo. This was Carrie's eighth surgery, and she knew the drill: Check in the night before the surgery for a series of blood tests. Once they were completed, an IV would be started—not an easy task given her small, delicate veins and pathetically thin and tiny arms.

I waved as I saw Carrie, but my approach was slowed by the densely packed room, filled with children and adults in various stages of distress. I noticed one child in particular, who appeared to be terrified, refusing to accompany his nurse to the ward. I watched as Carrie took his hand in hers and began to walk toward the ward with him. I followed, finally making it to the pair as they reached his assigned bed. "Hello, Dr. Perricone," Carrie said as I came into view. "This is Harry. I was just explaining to him how the IV works." I watched as Carrie carefully explained that once the needle was inserted it was easy to forget that it was even there. "In fact," she said proudly, "this will be my eighth time. Dr. Perricone, would it be okay if Harry watched me so he can see how easy it is?"

I forgot my fatigue in the face of Carrie's generosity of spirit and selflessness. An IV insertion is difficult at the best of times—and vastly more difficult with children.

Harry's face shone with hope and trust as he gazed at Carrie, whose courage and kindness accomplished what his parents and the highly trained medical staff could not. "I'll watch," said Harry, "and then it will be my turn."

Harry waited patiently while Carrie had her tests and got settled in her bed. As Harry watched, I inserted the IV in Carrie's arm. She smiled and chatted the whole time to Harry, never once flinching or otherwise indicating that the experience was unpleasant in any way.

Like fear, bravery can also be contagious. Harry's IV insertion went smoothly, and he wore it like a badge of courage. I could see in his face that he had undergone a profound change deep in his being. The fearful, cringing little boy had taken a first step toward becoming a man.

And it wasn't just Harry who underwent a heartfelt change of attitude. My self-pity at feeling that I had been through hell and back during the grueling hours of my internship receded into the netherworld. Carrie was a living embodiment of the spirit being stronger than the flesh, and I vowed to endure whatever hardships came my way with equal valor and dignity.

Carrie's final surgery was not a success. It was with great sadness that I learned of her death the following day. Although short, her life was not in vain. At least two other lives, both mine and Harry's, were irrevocably changed by Carrie's heroic spirit that stormy winter's night.

What I Learned

Perhaps the biggest mistakes I have made and observed made by others are those arising out of having the wrong perspective. Perspective is our own personal worldview, and it can be difficult to alter it. However, sometimes we get lucky and our perspectives can be radically shifted, resulting in positive life changes.

My perspective was that of an overworked intern who was perilously close to losing sight of the reason he had chosen a career in medicine. The selfless caring and love expressed by this little girl taught me what healing is really all about.

The lesson I learned was never to go through a day without reexamining my perspective, and this can be accomplished only by trying to see a situation through the eyes of others.

ALFRED MOLINA

Actor

I was not quite thirteen years old and my parents were halfway through a divorce. It was, to tell the truth, embarrassing. My mum and dad were Mediterranean, from Italy and Spain respectively. They were loud, and public, in their demonstrative, theatrical style of bickering. Name-calling was a specialty, one I have inherited and, to my shame, reduced myself to falling back on occasionally.

My solace was school, a bustling inner-city high school where anonymity was key to survival. I was able to disappear and be someone else. At school I was no longer Alfredo, the gangly, overweight son of a disappointed father and a mother whose emotional and creative horizons had dwindled to an obsession with food and daily assessments of how quickly she was aging. At school, I was Fred, and, more important, I could pretend and lie that I came from a stable family home where both parents lived in the bosom of each other's love. This lie, maintained over a period of years, became so much a part of my life that I was confident enough to create quirky details: nooks and crannies where, as in fiction, they could reside, uninvestigated and beyond reproach.

When my classmates spoke of their parents, either boastfully or otherwise, I was able to keep up, at least in my own mind, with an itinerary in my head (a complete fabrication) of what we had done over the weekend or during the holidays.

Most children of divorced parents create some kind of alternative family. Sometimes it takes the form of friends at school or work, and sometimes another family takes on a role as surrogates. In my case, I created another person, a happier, more confident person who, while denying the truth, forged a family that was actually not bad. I made excuses constantly for why only one or the other parent showed up for school events. As time went by the excuses became wilder and more exotic. As a consequence, I distanced my parents more and more from their actual lives, and from my own. We became strangers in a manner only sanctioned by intimacy. Once I had grown and moved away from the family home, the lies were no longer necessary.

As my parents belligerently succumbed to old age, I began to see them as they were: flawed, exasperating, individual, headstrong, loving, proud, and disarmingly human. My lies blinded me to these gifts of theirs.

WHAT I LEARNED

I denied myself the opportunity to know my parents at their most vulnerable, at the point of their greatest stress—perhaps, to tell the truth, when they needed me more than I needed them. My lies and the distance they caused were a big mistake.

CLAY DETTMER

Producer, *The Charles Grodin Show* on CNBC

It was graduation day at Yale in May of 1972. While sitting in a Gothic turret, I had my final heartfelt conversation with friend and roommate Alex Ponti (Carlo Ponti's son and Sophia Loren's stepson). Our backgrounds couldn't have been more diametrically opposed—he, the scion of Italian aristocracy, and I, a poor kid from a wildly dysfunctional family who had been given a full college scholarship. We spoke of the future and laughed heartily when he revealed his goal to go to med school and become anonymous and I revealed my goal to go to Hollywood and become famous.

Well, I never became famous, but I did attain a modicum of success as a working actor, mainly doing commercials and television. Nearly two decades into my career I read Charles Grodin's first book, *It Would Be So Nice if You Weren't Here,* a cautionary tale about his journey through show business. Chuck likened the prospects of pursuing an acting career as second only to selling poetry door-to-door!

About this time another classmate of mine, Geoff Taylor, was producing a movie for Disney called *Taking Care of Business,* starring Charles Grodin. Geoff had been admonishing me for years to find more gainful employment and offered me a production job as Charles Grodin's assistant. On the surface it seemed a risky pairing, putting me and Chuck together. After all, Chuck described himself as "low-key but high-strung" and later was fond of describing me as "high-key and high-strung!" But Geoff's instincts turned out to be right, as Chuck and I developed a very close personal and professional relationship.

I worked with Chuck for five years, making movies. He then signed on with CNBC to replace the departing Tom Snyder and do his own talk show. The natural progression for me was to move from California to New York and go from überassistant to television producer.

By the time I showed up at CNBC I was a fairly well developed free spirit. Based on my childhood on the streets, my college experience in the turbulent late 1960s and early 1970s, and my subsequent twenty-year career as an actor, I had pretty much perfected living life as a free agent. I had no problem questioning authority and had little patience for standing on ceremony. As such, it never dawned on me that my wearing a clean pair of sweats to work instead of, say, "a suit" would be a problem for anyone at the network. I did notice that more than one executive there said to me enviously, "I wish I could get away with that!" Yet it was many months, if not years, before I became aware that my dress was an issue . . . and here's how.

Evidently, Chuck had been getting some heat about my wardrobe. I'm sure Chuck couldn't have cared less how I dressed, but he certainly could do without the distraction. But it's not Chuck's style to be confrontational, especially on a seeming nonissue such as this. Knowing Chuck the way I did and having seen him in action over the years, I'd learned to listen for the subtext in what he said. He would indirectly get his point across, perhaps by telling a story with a moral involving a similar experience, or by simply "modeling" a certain behavior he might lead by example. Whenever Chuck would tell a story I would ask myself, *Is he trying to tell* me *something?*

I had been making periodic appearances on the show, usually comedic bits Chuck had dreamed up. When I mentioned going on a diet, Chuck jumped at the opportunity to have me do it on national television. I happily agreed, figuring rightly that it would give me added pressure to succeed. In hindsight I realize Chuck may have had additional motivation, and that was to get me into a pair of pants and thus get the "suits" off his back.

So I made biweekly appearances giving a progress report on my weight loss. On one such appearance the show's guest was Hugh Hefner. Chuck asked Hugh if he had seen the segment with his producer who wore sweats to work and what he thought of that. Hugh answered, "All of *my* executives come to work in bath-robes!"

The ultimate payoff came when I appeared thirty pounds lighter, looking good dressed in a pair of slacks and a Burberry coat and tie. The "new me" was met with applause and enthusiasm as Chuck gleefully put up stills of me fatter and in sweats to emphasize the before and after.

Chuck then asked me if he had seen the last of me in sweats, and I said, "Of course not!" I now understand the crestfallen look on his face.

Almost immediately I returned to my sweats, opting for comfort ahead of appearance. Chuck never mentioned the clothes issue again, and I assumed he felt that if it meant that much to me, he would live with it.

This attitude was in direct contrast to his attitude on another subject. He chose to personally pay my and another friend's salary out of his own pocket for years rather than have us report to the CNBC brass, whom he liked very much, but whose initial treatment of us he found unacceptable. But on the sweats he remained silent.

What I Learned

You can *always* do a better job for someone. Because I worked for and was paid by Charles Grodin Productions, the clothes police at the network had no authority over my attire. But if I ever do work with Chuck again, I won't be in sweats unless I'm *sure* it's okay with him, and since I haven't gotten thinner with age, it probably *would* be okay with him.

Incidentally, I'm able to wear sweats to work in my current position as a teacher in the Los Angeles Unified School District.

SHIRLEY MacLAINE

Academy Award–Winning Actress, Bestselling Author

So I said to Charles Grodin (Chuck, to those of us who have loved him for years), "What? You want me to write about my biggest mistakes? Goodness me, Chuck, I've spent my entire adult life writing about how there is no such thing as a mistake! But Chuck pressed me. Okay. Maybe the time I pulled a toy pistol on Sam Giancana and he reached for his .45 was a mistake. Or the time I kneed him in the balls because he twisted my arm so I'd eat his spaghetti. I don't know. A lot of guys with pinkie rings showed up ringside at my Vegas performances after that, so was it a mistake?

Maybe it was a mistake to purposely miss a train in the Soviet Union so I could smuggle myself into Leningrad University to observe anti-Catholic weeks. The Soviet state travel agency, Intourist, took my passport and stole my luggage. Okay, so I was stuck in Soviet Russia for a week, because I was then there illegally. But how could it be a mistake when I got to tell Brezhnev I would dance the cancan nude in Red Square every May Day if he didn't let me go home? I don't think that was really a mistake.

Was it a mistake for me to launch into metaphysical speculation about spirits who talk to God and extraterrestrials?

Goodness me, Chuck, even our president does that, except I think he's talking to an evildoer.

As a matter of fact, Chuck, why don't you call W. and ask him to contribute his biggest mistake. Do you have enough time?

I'll talk to God and ask him to wait.

What I Learned

Mistakes are "lessons in learning for growth."

PAUL RAGONESE

Retired Hero, New York City Police Officer

Claude "Danny" Richards was a New York City detective. In the mid-1980s I had worked with him on the Bomb Squad, and from 1998 to 2000 we worked together as private security at the New York Stock Exchange. At the NYSE we worked from six p.m. on Friday nights to six a.m. on Saturday mornings. Danny and I (he was still an active detective, but I had retired in 1988) were charged with searching the entire building and all entering vehicles for explosive devices with the assistance of explosive detective canines. When you work with someone for twelve hours on the overnight shift, conversations range from sports to religion to world events. We spent many nights solving the problems of the world and discussing whether Pete Rose should be inducted into the Baseball Hall of Fame.

Working on Wall Street and in the shadow of the World Trade Center, we spent numerous hours discussing the 1993 bombing and the incredible loss of life that would have resulted if the buildings had collapsed as planned by the terrorists. Danny had even commented on how we would be digging for over a year if that tragedy had occurred.

Danny was a special person. He was incredibly intelligent, caring, and compassionate. He had spent more than a year in Bosnia as a volunteer, helping to train and assist police in the war-torn country. He even spoke of returning, if it could be arranged. He was moved by the pain and suffering inflicted on the children and how they were deprived of the minimum needs of life, with no food, no clothing, and in many situations separated from their families. He was an expert on the political and social problems facing that country and educated me on what he felt should be done by America to help.

Danny, who was single, never had a bad word to say about anyone. Even when he was overlooked for a promotion, he never spoke badly of those detectives who had been given grade. "He has a wife and kids and can use the money," he would say, knowing full well that he was more deserving of the increase in pay and prestige. Many nights when I was exhausted from working my primary job during the day, we would get a call to search a vehicle at two a.m. and Danny would say to me, "Sit down and take a break. I'll take care of it."

On September 11, 2001, while off-duty and carrying an injured woman over his shoulder, Danny was killed when Tower 2 collapsed. I didn't hear about Danny's death even though I had volunteered to help in any small way I could at Ground Zero and at Fresh Kills Landfill. When I heard of his death I was hurt but not surprised. Anyone who knew him would expect him to act as heroically as he did, but the pain was still strong. Days turned to weeks and then months as the recovery operation continued. Danny's remains were not recovered. I went back to work and thought only of Danny, including him in my nightly prayers.

In the early spring of 2002 the recovery effort was still ongoing. My family and I were making preparations for Easter Sunday. On Holy Thursday evening I was in my bedroom when I bumped into an end table, flipping over a bowl containing numerous business cards that I had acquired over the years. One card fell to the floor, and I bent over and picked it up. It was Danny's NYPD card. I looked up and thought, *What do you want, buddy?* I smiled and went to bed.

I woke the next morning, which was Good Friday, and turned on the television as was my daily routine. The six a.m. news was just coming on and the anchor began the broadcast with "The remains

of another New York City police officer were recovered overnight."
The remains of Detective Claude Richards had been removed from
the vicinity of where Tower 2 once stood. I stared at the TV and
cried. It was as if Danny had told me the night before, "Hey, buddy,
they found me."

This incident has had a profound impact on my life and my religious beliefs. After September 11 I questioned how God could let
this happen. How could he allow so many innocent people to be
murdered? But after Danny was recovered, I understood that God
needed some more angels in heaven. Danny had gone home to God
and entered heaven to a welcome reserved for heroes. I am sure that
although he never received his detective promotion to first grade on
earth, First Grade Detective Claude "Danny" Richards is keeping
his eye on us while on patrol in a better place.

What I Learned

A man like Danny comes along so seldom. While I'm sure he was
aware how highly I thought of him, I wish I had been comfortable
enough to have told him so more openly. Male machismo seems to
prevent that. I learned never to leave any admiration or love unexpressed.

IRWIN REDLENER, MD

President and Cofounder, Children's Health Fund

It's not that I haven't made mistakes in my life; on the contrary, there have been more than I can remember. My problem is that many of these offenses of misjudgment, miscalculation, sloth, and simple stupidity are in one of two categories: far too embarrassing to reveal or completely devoid of any practical lesson to anyone—myself included.

More profound to me is the notion of a "near mistake." That's when we come perilously close to doing something truly regrettable but turn away and take a different course at the last minute. Experiences like this can be especially sobering, even poignant, as they remind us how fragile situations are. A turn here, a snap decision there, something important accepted or rejected at the last moment: all of these can have a profound impact on what happens in our lives.

My son Jason's life was a study in thrills. When he was a toddler and a young child it was about the excitement of running and exploring. Barriers were challenges and everything was entertaining—to himself as much as to the rest of us. And he laughed a lot. He laughed when he was running around and when he was fooling around with his siblings. He laughed at everybody's jokes—including his own. And he got away with murder, as people do when they are utterly charming and totally beautiful, as he had been from the moment he was born.

He more or less graduated from high school not that sure of what he would do. He went to Hunter College in New York and he went to Hawaii to learn how to make furniture from exotic koa wood. And I think he went there to meet part of his personal destiny, the lovely Sheareen. She was blond and smart and liked big dreams. Perfect for each other. They came back to New York and eventually married. Koa wood furniture was not in high demand in NYC circa 1995, so Jason began renovating apartments in New York and Philadelphia.

When they made enough money to support their real dream, Jason and Sheareen headed west. Karen and I were in New York and had loved having them "in the neighborhood." They, on the other hand, were both deeply into the world of aggressive X-gen sports: snowboarding, mountain biking, and skateboarding. So why not go to Mecca? Indeed. And in 1998, ground zero for this lifestyle was a pristine town at the base of Mount Bachelor—Bend, Oregon. They knew no one there but were totally exhilarated by finding this place, their place, and starting a new life. My God, they were in love, and they were overwhelmed with anticipation.

When they got to Bend, this was the plan: Jason would build Sheareen a store (she wanted to sell "New York fashions" for teenage girls in their new community) and, once the store was built, he would spend a few months trying to figure out what he would do next. And while he was at it, he would absorb the environment, wallowing in the wonders of that extraordinary atmosphere from the seat of his souped-up mountain bike in the mornings and on a snowboard in the bowls of Mount Bachelor in the afternoons.

All of this was an incredible adventure for the lovebirds. For our part, Karen and I were truly happy for them—mostly. In fact, we were actually thrilled when murmurs of having children began to surface, and we got into serious "grandparent-think." We were, on the other hand, a little disconcerted at the gradual realization that they planned to stay out west—and, worse, they were starting to think about a second store for Sheareen. And this time, they were talking Hawaii. Yikes. I just didn't deal with this well. Not at all. But the more I laid a guilt trip on Jason, the less he felt like speaking to me. Phone calls became increasingly tense—and less frequent. Our relationship was not, as they say, in a good place.

And there it stood, for a few crucial months. My relationship with this wonderful twenty-eight-year-old adventurer, dreamer, philosopher, risk taker, sweetheart, was on ice—and it was terrible.

It might have remained there, but I decided that we would visit Jason and Sheareen. Karen and I would go to Bend, see where they lived, see the new store, and just hang out. I tell you, it was wonderful—more than we could have hoped for in so many ways. We laughed and cried and played and talked. That was it. The little problem we were having—now fixed. That was in August of 1998.

On March 27, 1999, Jason was snowboarding off-trail in a fresh powder bowl. The sky was crystalline, a bright sun shining on the mountain overlooking Bend. Sheareen was waiting for him at the base. Some hikers in the distance had their eyes on Jason, a random boarder on the far decline of the bowl. No trees in sight, no boulders or obstructions. And Jason, a tremendously talented and very careful athlete, was making his turns in the fresh snow. Then, it seems, the tip of his board caught on some unseen branch or snow-covered rock. He flipped and spun over, landing on his abdomen. He lay there in the snow, bleeding internally, waiting for the distant observers to call for help, waiting for the rescue teams to find him and call for evacuation.

He was still alive when they reached him, but not for long. A week later one of the members of the rescue team told me his last words were "I'm sorry, Dad."

Years later, the pain is there—and will stay there—for every living soul who ever met Jason. For Karen and me, for Jason's mom and his brothers and sister, the loss is unspeakable.

Yet I have often, very often, thought of how much worse it *almost* was. What if we hadn't made amends, reconciled our "differences of opinion" over whatever? Where they would live and how inconvenient it might be to visit them? Preposterous. I would simply never have forgiven myself if we hadn't made that visit months before Jason died.

So, this was *almost* a monumentally terrible mistake.

WHAT I LEARNED

Fundamentally, this was the most profound lesson I have learned in life. It is about the necessity to attend to the relationships that are of deep and abiding importance to us. The relationships that matter most must be cherished and nurtured. When they fall off track, they need to be fixed with compassion—and haste. I have learned much from my own "close call." I now think about all of my relationships virtually every day. None of us is perfect, of course, and none can know when the worst will happen. But the very last thing we want is deep regret that can't be fixed, because time steadfastly refuses to be rolled back, no matter how many tears a human being sheds.

PAUL NEWMAN

Actor, Director, Food Impresario

I've never learned from my mistakes. I thought I had, but the mistakes that I made sixty years ago, I still make today. Joanne will back me up on this. Actually, there's something quite enjoyable about making the same mistakes. You're never surprised; you are only disheartened—there's some comfort in that. I understand Woody Allen feels the exact same way. In fact, he wrote a long article about this in the *New York Times,* which I didn't read because I knew it would cover familiar ground. I've been asked to write stuff like this before, which, as you can see, is the same old mistake.

What I Learned

Nothing!

Acknowledgments

My editor at Springboard, Karen Murgolo, was so easy to work with, along with somehow always seeming to be cheerful. My agent, Eileen Cope of Trident Media, was dedicated and always had a strong belief in this book. Karen Murgolo's worthy assistant, Tom Hardej, was sensitive, kind, and right on top of everything. Sarah Parrish at HELP USA was invaluable, as was my assistant, Rose Snyder. Two very nice ladies.

Some of the contributors were particularly helpful in reaching out to other contributors. A big thanks to Susan Ungaro, Bill Dana, Bob Ellis, John Gabriel, Rich Martini, Kenneth Cole, Shelly Schultz, Alan and Arlene Alda, and Gene Wilder.

Also, Matilda Cuomo, Maria Cuomo Cole, and Scott Smith were devoted allies.

Thanks to all.

Copyrights

Index to Contributors

About Charles Grodin

CHARLES GRODIN is a recent recipient of the William Kuntsler Award for racial justice. He is credited with gaining clemency for four women in prison under New York's Rockefeller Drug Laws, and was noted by New York's governor George Pataki for helping to get those laws reformed. He is also a recent recipient of the HELP Hero Award for his humanitarian efforts on behalf of the homeless.

Mr. Grodin is best known as a movie actor (*The Heartbreak Kid*, *Midnight Run*, and the *Beethoven* movies are among his many films). He has written five books, including the bestseller *It Would Be So Nice if You Weren't Here*, and received an Emmy Award for writing the 1977 *Paul Simon Special*. He is currently a commentator for CBS News and was nominated for the New York Festivals 2007 Radio Broadcasting Lifetime Achievement Award.

All of Mr. Grodin's proceeds from this book go to HELP USA, one of the nation's largest providers of services for the homeless.